GARDEN LIBRARY
PLANTING FIELDS ARBORETUM

D1035349

GARDEN LIBRARY
PLANTING FIELDS ARBORETUM

ROYAL GARDENS *of* EUROPE

Contents

Introduction

Royal gardeners have always been a privileged group. Wealthy beyond most of their subjects' wildest dreams, through successive centuries of European history from the Middle Ages until the 20th century, they enjoyed enormous — in some cases unlimited — power. That power manifested itself in a variety of ways, but one thing it certainly brought with it was patronage over the arts. At the same time kings, queens, and ruling princes realized that visible evidence of their elevated positions was crucial to maintaining the perception of their status. Through the Middle Ages this showed itself rather crudely in castles and fortified towns. From the Renaissance on, however, cultural patronage and innovation became of increasing significance. For many monarchs, building palaces and surrounding them with impressive gardens was one of the best ways of providing such evidence of both their power and their prestige. Within these glittering settings the ceremony and entertainment of court life could be carried out.

The foundations of the modern European garden were laid in Italy during the unprecedented creative period of the Renaissance and the patrons of these gardens, as in all areas of the arts, were powerful, wealthy families in the various Italian states. As the development of gardens moved to other European countries, such as Belgium, England, France, Germany, the Netherlands, Portugal, and Spain in particular, the active involvement of royalty became increasingly significant. For over two hundred years, through the 17th and 18th centuries and well into the 19th, monarchs and rulers all over the Continent played the leading part in the development of gardens. With the exception of the English landscape movement of the 18th century, for which the primary patrons were the wealthy Whig aristocrats who dominated English politics and society at the time, European monarchs were prime movers in the development of all the major styles of garden design, from French classical to Dutch baroque and German rococo.

This dominant position in the development of gardens was facilitated by dynastic connexions through marriage and family, and through the ability of the monarchs to use their positions to ensure they gained access to the network of leading designers, architects, craftsmen, and plantsmen. These two reasons were fundamental to the widespread influence of Versailles. As well as wishing to emulate what was acknowledged by the end of the 17th century to be the most magnificent royal garden in Europe, the royal garden-makers often had direct connections with Louis XIV. His grandson, Philip V followed his example with his gardens in Spain at Aranjuez and La Granja, as did Philip's son and Louis' great-grandson, Charles III, with his garden at Palazzo Reale in Italy. And as Louis XIV had used his royal power to ensure he took on the services of the trio responsible for the most distinguished forerunner to Versailles in France, Vaux-le-Vicomte, so other European monarchs either took on men who had worked at Versailles — notably Peter the Great with his employment of Jean-Baptiste Le Blond, the most accomplished pupil of Versailles' designer, André Le Nôtre. If the monarchs were not able to take on men who had actually worked at Versailles, they ensured that their designers were well acquainted with the gardens.

Louis XIV's successor, Louis XV, donated statues to Frederick the Great for his garden at Sanssouci, and the Prussian king himself had regular gardening discussions and comparisons with his sister who was married to the King of Sweden and who made notable additions to the garden of

Drottningholm. Such family relationships through marriage abounded in the various German states and beyond, although they were not always primarily cordial; the garden-making of successive generations of the Bourbon and Habsburg rulers of Spain, Austria, and the Italian kingdom of Sicily and Naples was more often driven by competitive hostility. Friendly or not, however, the dynastic evolution of different European countries ensured that single families often had an influence in more than one country. In addition to the Bourbons and Habsburgs, William of Orange and his wife Mary, daughter of King James II of England, played key roles in the development of the leading royal gardens in both the Netherlands and England at the time, Het Loo and Hampton Court. The Hanoverian dynasty that ruled England on the death of Queen Anne in 1714 would later encourage the spread of English gardening styles to its native principality in Germany.

Various members of the Hanoverian family in England were among those who demonstrated the powerful and innovative horticultural and botanical networks that European royal gardeners were in a position to establish. The Royal Botanic Garden, Kew, was begun in the mid-18th century from two adjacent royal homes and parks, Richmond and Kew House. King George II and his wife Queen Caroline lived

OPPOSITE LEFT
An engraving of William and Mary (Dutch School, c.1688–94), king and queen first in the Netherlands and then in England. Together they created gardens in both countries, notably at Het Loo and at Hampton Court.

OPPOSITE RIGHT
Queen Elizabeth the Queen Mother in the protected walled garden of her private home, the Castle of Mey, in the far north of Scotland. She created other gardens at official royal residences, but this was always her favourite.

ABOVE
Part of the intricate formal parterres at Het Loo in the Netherlands where the original garden begun under William and Mary was painstakingly restored during the 1980s to accurately recreate the original.

at Richmond while their son Frederick, Prince of Wales, and his wife Princess Augusta lived at Kew. After Frederick's early death Augusta continued his garden assisted by the statesman and keen gardener, Lord Bute, and established a modest botanic garden in 1759. After her death, by which time George III had become king, he joined the two properties together and developed the botanic gardens. He was advised by Lord Bute and Sir Joseph Banks as an unofficial director. After the death of Banks in 1820, as well as that of the king, the personal royal connection with Kew diminished, and in 1838 the garden was transferred into the national botanical institution.

The early plant-collecting expeditions carried out by men sent by Kew were working on behalf of their royal patrons, and when the first collector, Francis Masson, returned to England in the 1770s, after collecting in the Cape Colony of South Africa for Kew, he named the most exotic plant that he

returned with, *Strelitzia regina*, in honour of George III's wife. Less than a century later, by which time Kew had become the most prestigious horticultural establishment in the world, the reigning monarch, Queen Victoria, was similarly honoured with the name of one of the most impressive new plants to be introduced from South America to the botanic garden's glasshouses, *Victoria amazonica*.

Victoria and her husband, Prince Albert, focused their attention on the gardens of their favourite homes, in particular Osborne House on the Isle of Wight, and this was the case for future members of the English royal family. Queen Elizabeth the Queen Mother was especially fond of her home and garden at the Castle of Mey in Scotland and she undoubtedly sparked a love of gardening in her grandson, the present Prince of Wales, which he has expressed in the garden of his own private home, Highgrove House, in Gloucestershire.

LEFT
*The fabulous display
of fountains and gilded
statues in the main
cascade at Peterhof,
Russia, a garden created
by Peter the Great
expressly to celebrate
Russia's military victories
and emergence as a
European power.*

RIGHT
*Catherine the Great
by Vladimir Lukic
Borovikovski, a portrait
of the empress with her
greyhound at Tsarskoye
Selo where she introduced
the landscape garden
to Russia and celebrated
her cultural attachment
to England.*

The gardens described in this book confirm time and again the degree to which successive royal patrons were able to benefit from outstanding expertise, and the royal gardens created in Russia around St Petersburg are ideal examples. We have already seen how Peter the Great secured for himself the skills of the Versailles-trained Jean-Baptiste Le Blond, and in similar fashion his granddaughter-in-law, Catherine the Great, imported the necessary skills to achieve her desired English landscapes. The work that the Scottish-born architect carried out for her as decorator, architect, and landscape designer at Tsarskoye Selo and Pavlovsk represent one of the most significant essays in classical architecture and landscape gardening anywhere in Europe during the 18th century.

Gardens of the highest quality could be achieved by using royal power and patronage to employ the best possible designers and craftsmen. This could also be helped by royal inheritance, as demonstrated in the case of the Austrian Archduke Franz Ferdinand and his garden at Konopiste in Bohemia. The quality of his garden's ornamental decoration increased enormously with his inheritance through his mother, sister of the King of Sicily and Naples, of the collection of the Duke of Modena, in particular the statuary that had decorated the gardens of the Villa d'Este, which came into the Modena's family collection after its removal from d'Este during the 18th century.

Certainly such decorative quality has been a trademark of royal gardens through the centuries and given them a certain stamp that sets them apart in a small elite. Outstanding and original plantsmanship becomes a feature in some of the gardens from the 19th century onwards, but both before and afterwards the architectural and sculptural skills and the materials used make them, as a group, almost unique repositories of garden architecture and decorative ornament. The developing evolution of the gardens and their survival is mostly due to the continuity they have enjoyed from one generation to another. In many of the gardens the original design was adapted, added to, or expanded on more than one occasion by succeeding generations of the same family. In a minority of cases the original garden disappeared or was altered beyond all recognition, but these were rare. More often the end result over centuries was a garden that has grown in layers that are both individual and interrelated.

For the gardens' survival in modern times the privilege of royal status has been paramount. It has ensured that soaring costs of maintenance have been met, in particular in those cases where ownership has passed from a royal family to the state. It has also led to a series of restorations, and some of these such as at Het Loo, Hampton Court, and Peterhof are among the most ambitious and meticulous garden reconstructions ever carried out. But while these gardens are no longer private royal property, at others the royal families maintain this continuity; some three centuries after their creation the gardens of Drottningholm, Fredensborg, and Aranjuez, for instance, are still enjoyed by the respective Swedish, Danish, and Spanish royal families.

While some of the grandest gardens created centuries ago have been adapted to provide the privacy sought in today's modern world, to find that privacy has been the driving force in the creation of the contemporary gardens from the 20th century onwards. At Drottningholm and Fredensborg public access is combined with a degree of privacy for the royal families who use the palaces as their official residences. But other gardens around private homes, such as Highgrove and Château de Belvédère, have quite different and far more personal atmospheres. Here, garden-loving owners are able to create the gardens they want and grow their favourite plants, with some spectacular results. In both cases, outstanding contemporary garden designers and craftsmen have been commissioned to assist and so continue the centuries-old tradition of quality.

Given the age of many of the gardens and the variety of their characteristics, there are some suitable for more than one of the various chapters. But they have been grouped according to where their primary features are best suited, so although Peterhof would no longer be surviving in its glittering state if it were not for prodigious restoration after World War II, it remains in essence the show garden Peter the Great had in mind when it was created in the 18th century. Osborne House

OPPOSITE
A vista in the gardens of Belvédère, Belgium, where formal designs are enhanced by plantings of outstanding botanical and horticultural interest.

LEFT
Japanese azaleas in brilliant springtime bloom in the Valley Gardens, Windsor Great Park, Surrey. They were created along with the adjacent Savill Gardens by royal initiative from the 1930s to the 1950s.

was purchased and developed by Queen Victoria and her husband Prince Albert specifically to be their private country house where they could relax away from the public gaze. The gardens were expertly restored in the 1990s and replanted. But it is as a horticultural and garden-design period piece that perhaps makes it most intriguing.

The gardens reveal many different connexions weaved into their creation and development: of friendship and family, admiration for a design style, or use of designers, architects, sculptors, and craftsmen, who either worked at other gardens discussed in this book or were trained by men who did. As a group they form a unique illustration of garden making in Europe through more than four centuries and a showcase for the Continent's extraordinary gardening heritage from the Renaissance to the 21st century. It must be hoped that the achievements will continue in the future, not just with maintenance and restoration of existing gardens, but also with the addition of exciting new ones that will draw on contemporary gardening styles of the future as well as fitting into the historical tapestry to which they belong.

In recent decades almost all of the gardens discussed have been made accessible to visitors and have proved themselves to be among the most popular in the world. This alone augurs well for their future.

GARDENS
FOR DISPLAY

By the beginning of the 17th century European nations and states, both large and small, were totally dominated by monarchies. At the same time the influence of the Renaissance was spreading rapidly throughout the Continent. The result was an incentive for patronage of the arts that Europe's rulers were quick to take up, not least because it increased perception of their status and power.

Despite the disputes between different countries and dynasties that ensured regular wars through the 17th and 18th centuries, the position and prestige of monarchies was undiminished until the French Revolution (1789–95) shook the foundations of royal authority. In the two centuries before then royal patronage flowered as never before or since and, given the revolution in gardens and the perception of them brought about by the Renaissance, they came to high prominence.

Whether absolute rulers of major nations with empires, such as Louis XIV of France or the Holy Roman Emperors in Vienna, or monarchs of smaller states as in Denmark and parts of Germany, they were all positioned at the apex of political

and social life that revolved around the court. The gardens they created were primarily places to provide the setting for court life and also to make a statement to admiring observers, as was demonstrated most memorably at Louis XIV's Versailles. Members of the French court and the numerous visitors from other European nations were left in no doubt whatsoever that the French king's primary intention was to create a display that confirmed his royal position. Any horticultural or botanical qualities, which would come to the fore in future gardens of the 19th and 20th centuries, were almost purely recreational as we can see in the chapter The Age of Leisure (pp. 40–75). Much more important was the creation of a formal landscape that provided the framework for an ornamental display in which the two crucial ingredients, water and statuary, were used to create a story.

It was perhaps not surprising that the most powerful monarchs with huge wealth, such as Louis XIV, were able to have such lavish gardens. But their importance as a reflection of royal prestige is equally confirmed by the manner in which the example was taken throughout Europe in countries large and small. They confirmed that horticulture was often not the prime incentive: gardens were created to celebrate military victories, as in the case of Peter the Great's Peterhof (see pp. 30–5), but also purely as a celebration of royal prestige and

OPPOSITE
At Palazzo Reale, Caserta, Italy, the spectacular landscape was used in a unique fashion as a backdrop to a formal garden.

LEFT
Les Bosquets, *a painting of Versailles c.1720, by Jean-Baptiste Martin, pseudonym Martin des Batailles, illustrates how the lavish nature of the garden with fountains and rows of Classical statues was matched by the* fêtes champêtres *and other court events that took place here.*

PREVIOUS PAGES
A domed rotunda perfectly positioned overlooking water in the garden of Nymphenburg, Germany, where a series of outstanding buildings adorn the areas on either side of the central baroque design.

patronage, as seen in Queluz in Portugal (*see pp.26–9*). Whatever the particular inspiration, the result was universal – a dazzling and impressive celebration.

One important feature, which provides a recurring theme through the book, is that gardens are never static; however architectural, they have a natural tendency to evolve. The Versailles gardens have remained relatively unchanged in their major features, but for others the original layout has been added to, and many have undergone extensive, in some cases, total restoration. At Nymphenburg (*see pp.22–5*), for instance, several of the outstanding buildings are now found in parts of the garden that were developed in the landscape style in the late 18th and early 19th centuries (*see pp.12–13*), and at

Wilanów in Poland (*see pp.96–9*), while the garden was originally created for display, its later landscaping is its most lasting quality. In this light a number of the gardens discussed qualify for more than one of the chapters. Wilanów, which is looked at in detail in a later chapter, is one example. Another is Peterhof which would not be in existence but for the post-war restoration, and yet its overriding *raison d'être* and appearance revolve around the display that was originally responsible for its creation. The gardens are also of a period when European monarchs not only felt confident and powerful enough to display their royal position, but realized that such visible signs were an important part of the perception of royalty.

Versailles

VERSAILLES · FRANCE

The principal reason for the creation of the gardens at Versailles, which spanned nearly 25 years, beginning in 1661 when Louis XIV came to the throne, was to provide a visible symbol of the monarch's absolute authority. In his study of the history of French gardens, *Princely Gardens*, Kenneth Woodbridge concludes that Versailles "has assumed an importance in the history of French gardening proportional to the political significance which attached to it as a symbol of the French monarchy." The Thirty Years' War had ended and Louis was indisputably the most powerful man in Europe. While that position would fluctuate during his long reign, his style of divine authority was never in question in France. At Versailles, for the first time in history, a garden would be used as visible evidence of royal power, and it was for this reason that it was planned on such a large and grandly detailed scale and would immediately become the model for ambitious royal garden-makers all over Europe.

Shortly after Louis came to the throne he decided that he wanted to move his court from the metropolitan Louvre palace to somewhere, as the garden historian Pierre-André Leblaude has described, "that could accommodate his large retinue and provide some insulation from the annoyances of

ABOVE RIGHT
The heroic scale and style of the palace's architecture, encapsulated by the sculpture groups adorning the roofscape, is matched by the spread of parterres around the façades and the areas of garden beyond.

RIGHT
A perspective view of Versailles by Pierre Patel, dated 1668, shows the palace and gardens at an early stage of their development. The gardens in front of the king's and queen's apartments are to the left and right of the main building, beyond Le Nôtre's main axis.

urban life". Versailles was one of his father's hunting-lodges, and despite it being in unprepossessing, flat countryside, he was fond of it, and it became his chosen location. He had the political inspiration to make a grand statement and the perfect challenge to the château of Vaux-le-Vicomte, which had recently been created by his brilliant finance minister, Nicolas Fouquet. The minister's intention to impress his king backfired; after visiting Vaux-le-Vicomte for a glittering fête, Louis decided that his minister had overreached himself. Fouquet was arrested and later imprisoned for life.

The connexion with Vaux-le-Vicomte was not just one of jealous inspiration. It provided the key craftsmen who were to create the gardens, in particular André Le Nôtre, who would be responsible for the layout of the site, which extended to nearly 8sq km (3sq m). Louis took on Louis Le Vau, the architect who would carry out the first two extensions that transformed Versailles from a hunting-lodge to a palace, to be completed by a third extension by Jules Hardouin-Mansart, and the sculptor Charles Le Brun. The whole project was controlled by Fouquet's replacement, Jean-Baptiste Colbert.

The Vaux-le-Vicomte gardens were never on the scale that Le Nôtre was to develop at Versailles, but they provided the crucial opportunity for him to reveal the powerful message of formal symmetry. At Versailles the task was initially challenging, with thick woods crowded close to the château, and there was little rise or fall in the land to create perspective. He overcame the problems by building great terraces on which intricately patterned or water parterres were laid out and by expanding the garden away from the château. For the new apartments he made the Parterre de L'Amour to the south in front of Queen Marie Thérèse's rooms and the Parterre du Nord in front of Louis's windows on the north side. From these beginnings the gardens expanded again, in particular to the north and west, in a series of sweeping axial designs. The largest and most memorable was to the west, where by the late 1660s the enormous canal was being dug.

Formally controlled water was to be a defining feature of Le Nôtre's gardens at Versailles, and the *bassins*, fountains, and canals were always integral to the message that the gardens conveyed. The fountains had their own architect and a resident chief fountainier whose stern responsibilities were outlined in Colbert's *Règlement pour les fontaines de Versailles*: "The master-fountainer Denis must always have three assistant plumbers and six boys as is specified in his contract. They will all lodge in the pump building according to the allocation which will be made. None of the said assistants may lodge anywhere else

on pain of dismissal from the service. None of them shall be taken off duty without giving us notice." The flat terrain and constant mechanical problems would later make it impossible for the increasing quantities of fountains to work together at once and would eventually lead to the construction of the monstrous Machine de Marly, a series of huge waterwheels that raised water from the Seine and pumped it uphill into reservoirs. It never solved the problem completely, however, and when either the king or other important guests were going round the gardens a series of boys with whistles alerted each other when successive fountains should be activated as they approached and turned off after they had moved away. But whatever the problems, Le Nôtre knew that water could enliven the enormous scale of his gardens, and the creations at Versailles would provide a lesson followed in different parts of Europe for over a century.

The other essential ingredient to the Versailles gardens was the programme of sculpture. The fact that it was overseen by Le Brun, who chose subjects and executed drawings with a team of between 40 and 50 sculptors, gives an idea of the scale of the work. Using the most sumptuous materials possible, including white marble, bronze, and gilded bronze, the sculptors created vases and urns, statues to be positioned in long sentinel lines on plinths along vistas and avenues, and lavish figure groups for fountain basins on a scale never witnessed before or since in any one single garden. And the sculpture was not purely decorative – its key purpose was to tell a story and to portray a grand narrative that showed Louis XIV in his absolute position. Central to this was Louis's identification with Apollo, the sun god, created in particular in the great west axis of the canal, focusing on the Bassin d'Apollon. The king's relationship with the deities of the ancient world was added to by more temporal representations: the continents of the world, the seasons, and the rivers of France, for instance, and the overall effect was an architectural decorative scheme whose sumptuousness was matched by the significance of the iconography.

Allied to the elements of display in the gardens was the underlying importance of the occasions for which they were designed. This was never a garden for the king to enjoy in his private leisure, rather it was to act as the backcloth for a glittering court life that visibly demonstrated the richness and power of the monarchy. The contemporary engravings of the gardens almost invariably depict quantities of people

ABOVE
The enormity of Versailles is encapsulated in this panoramic view across the Bassin de Latone between the Parterre d'Eau and the Tapis Verts, with the main western vista stretching away into the distance.

LEFT
A gilded statue in one of the fountain basins at Versailles exemplifies the quality of craftsmanship at the palace. The combination of the beautiful figures and water gives a great sense of movement.

in the gardens, in many instances at a fête, banquet, or other celebration, some of which lasted for many days. Leblaude described one of the most magnificent fêtes of all, held on 18 July 1668 to celebrate the signing of the Treaty of Aix-la-Chapelle. The fête cost 117,000 livres for one day, as Leblaude says: "more than a third of what was spent that year in work on the building and gardens".

In his words: "The July 1668 fête followed the same general lines as that in 1664 but this time all the activities were packed into a single day. There were new temporary architectural settings and open-air glades at the intersection of the paths. After a light meal offered at the Bosquet d'Etoile, guests walked down to the old Rondeau, where they were entertained by swans floating in and out of fountain spray before turning and walking back up the slope towards an amphitheatre set up on the site of the future Bassin de Saturne, one of the four pools dedicated to the Seasons. Here the magnificent tapestries from the royal collections merged into the surrounding greenery. Twisted columns of false marble and lapis lazuli alternated with statues of Peace and Victory, framing a ten metre stage lit by crystal chandeliers. The canvas backdrop depicted an illusionistic view of the walk directly behind it, which led to the orangery."

Molière gave his first performance of *George Dandin* to an audience of 1200; afterwards supper was served "five courses each of 56 dishes" in a temporary salon, and then there was a ball in an area decorated with rockwork and fountains.

Finally, "the guests contemplated the gardens lit up by thousands of tiny lights, before the huge final explosion of fireworks and rockets outlined the king's monogram in the night sky."

What visitors to Versailles were witnessing was a display of royal authority combined with the supremacy of French gardens. By the time Le Nôtre had finished his work, perhaps his overriding achievement was the demonstration of man's control over nature with the clear message that such authority represented royal power. Whether in the alignment of the parterres, *allées*, and canals, or the series of intricate *bosquets*, the whole landscape became not only planned, but ordered. It was a deliberate move away from the Italian celebration of man's harmonious relationship with nature to being in control. In the words of the garden historian Victor Tapie, "the gardens outside the palace form another composition to which the word 'architecture' is also fitting, to such an extent does the order of the *miroirs d'eau*, the terraces, the elegant caprice in the design of the parterres, the canal wide as a river, seem necessary there."

Such a dazzling display conveying such a powerful message was not lost on Louis's contemporaries and successive garden makers. Nothing would ever match the court of Versailles at its zenith, but gardens created to provide the setting for a royal court and a demonstration of royal authority, using a combination of artistic, architectural, and landscaping elements, would remain as an unrivalled representation of what royal supremacy represented.

ABOVE

Apollo's chariot arises from the water in one of the most symbolic episodes in the iconography at Versailles, representing the rising sun and paying homage to the sun god.

RIGHT

An engraving of the Machine de Marly at Bougival, where a mechanism of 14 waterwheels forced some 5000 cubic m (176,575 cubic ft) daily over 150m (500ft) up the hillside to feed the aqueduct to Versailles.

LEFT

Sentinel-like statues of Classical deities are executed to exquisite standards of craftsmanship. The brilliance of their white marble is enhanced by the background of clipped green foliage.

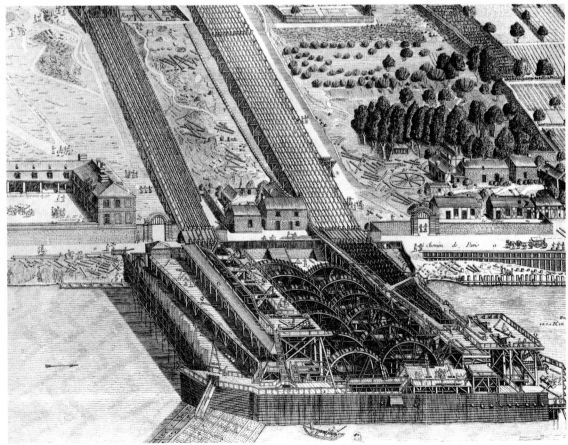

Nymphenburg

MUNICH · GERMANY

One garden that was originally envisaged, if not eventually executed, on a scale to rival Versailles was the garden of Nymphenburg, home of the Electors of Bavaria in Munich. The palace was begun during the 1660s at the same time as Versailles, but it was later that aspirations of rivalry were to emerge. Initially, the inspiration was also driven by non-gardening events, as the garden historian C.I. Robert has described: "The Thirty Years' War had, to all intents and purposes, destroyed the nation's Renaissance civilization and dissipated the means of reconstruction. After 1660, as after 1918, the national imagination was fired by the ideal of reconstruction." The impetus for the gardens and palace came in 1654 when Elector Ferdinand Maria married the Italian Princess Adelaide of Savoy, who was to make the Bavarian court, and Nymphenburg as its home, one of the most brilliant places in Europe.

Adelaide's Italian architect, Agostino Barelli designed the new palace that forms the central block of the building today,

BELOW
An 18th-century engraving of the principal parterre at Nymphenburg showing it in a state of youthful grandeur.

OPPOSITE
The chaste splendour of the palace's main façade is enhanced by the spaciousness of the formal garden in front, which extends into the garden's long central axis and the main canal.

but the gardens were primarily the work of her son, Max Emanuel. For a number of years he served as Governor of the Spanish Netherlands, which gave him first-hand experience of Dutch gardens. Having succeeded as Elector, he was forced into exile for eleven years and lived in Paris where he studied French gardens, on his return to Munich he was determined to create a garden at Nymphenburg to rival Versailles. As Louis XIV had taken his main craftsmen from Vaux-le-Vicomte, so Emanuel took two architects with him from France, Charles Carbonet and Dominique Girard, the latter of whom had worked at Versailles.

As at Versailles, the flatness of the site at Nymphenburg was overcome by the enormous scale of the formal garden, in particular by the main central axis running east-west across the palace, which spread out into broad wings and courtyards – the width of the buildings accentuating at right-angles the power of the garden axis along which ran the main canal. At one distant point from the palace a vast flow of water pours over the grand cascade, decorated – as were the gardens throughout – by magnificent white marble statues. In front of the main west facade of the palace an enormous *parterre de broderie* was laid out, and the main central canal was supplemented by a network of smaller ones, adding to the garden's overall design. But in addition to the main central vista, perhaps Emmanuel's most inspired addition at Nymphenburg was the series of garden buildings that he commissioned, each surrounded by its own formal garden. One, the Pagodenburg, was built in oriental style and was used as a dressing and rest room by the actors and actresses who put on plays in the outdoor theatre to entertain the court; two more were the Magdalenenklause hermitage and Badenburg bathing house. Later, Emanuel's son Karl Albrecht made an exquisite addition to the garden buildings when he commissioned the pink-and-white Amalienburg as a hunting lodge for his wife, Maria Amalia.

By the late 18th century the grand displays of Nymphenburg had been captured by the renowned artist Bernardo Bellotto and commented on by numerous visitors, including von Rothenstein, who said: "The garden has 19 fountains, which give out 285 jets; and such a number of water-devices, gilt vases and statues meet the eye that they are better imagined than described. The great flower-parterre is 138 fathoms in length, and has one large fountain, four smaller ones, and a six-headed one…. On the edge of the tank, on the border round it, there are 8 gilt frogs, spurting water upwards in arches. This grand fountain cost 60,000 guilden, and used 250 cwt. of lead. Then you come to another great tank which has 6 springs all in a row. And into this basin the canal runs right and left, passing onward to the great cascade."

Having suffered the indignity of losing his kingdom and being forced into exile, when he returned to Germany Emanuel used the creation of Nymphenburg as a display of his restored position and authority as the ruler of Bavaria. As at Versailles, the combination of architecture and superlative craftsmanship in the statues, buildings, and other ornaments heightened the impact of the overall scale. Even though much of the formal garden was landscaped during the late 18th and early 19th century, the key formal features were retained. Looking back to the palace from the cascade at the far end of the long canal makes it easy to appreciate the sheer size and grandeur of the original scheme.

ABOVE
An engraving of the Mall at Nymphenburg, one of the architectural ornaments shown in its original formal setting; it was subsequently softened into more natural lines in the 18th-century changes.

BELOW
The cascade at the far end of the main canal continues the formal garden's breathtaking scale, both in the luxurious flow of water and the size of the marble statues of river gods.

RIGHT
From the baroque grandeur of the main formal gardens Nymphenburg offers surprise discoveries in the wooded areas on both sides, such as the figure of Pan above a rocky cascade.

Palácio de Queluz

QUELUZ · PORTUGAL

Portugal in the mid-18th century was, as had been the case before and continued to be afterwards, on the periphery of European culture, less affected than other places by changes in fashion and dependent upon its own traditions. But in the middle of the 18th century the Portuguese royal family, the Braganzas, used the gardens around their palace of Queluz to display an exotic vibrancy to rival most others in Europe.

After the original manor house had been transformed into the present baroque palace, the future king, Pedro III, turned to the French architect Jean-Baptiste Robillon to take over the work and create the surrounding gardens. He combined the baroque formality of intricate parterres enclosed by balustraded terraces with a dramatic use of statuary and divided an area of ornamental woodland lying beyond by a

LEFT
The garden combines the Classical influence from other European countries, illustrated by this marble figure of a woman and child, with the unique Portuguese decoration of painted tiles.

ABOVE
The Fountain of Nereid is the focal point on the far side of the Garden of Neptune from the central façade of the palace. The main area is filled with a geometric box-hedged parterre.

network of carriage drives and paths enlivened by fountains. Immediately in front of the palace the two main parterres, the Garden of Neptune and the Garden of Malta, were laid out side by side with patterns of clipped box and gravel and symmetrically arranged statues. The Garden of Malta was used for the entertainment of foreign ambassadors. The Garden of Neptune is dominated by two fountain basins, the first the Fountain of Neptune with a group of Poseidon and Athena in the centre, and the second, the Fountain of the Nereid, showing the sea-nymph Thetis (with whom Poseidon fell in love) rising from the waves bearing trays of jewels made for her by Hephaestus. The originality of the statuary continues with the variety of figures surrounding the basins and elsewhere, such as the lead sea serpent coiled around a stone

ball and spouting water into the Fountain of Neptune, or a pair of white marble sphinxes with women's heads and lions' bodies, dressed in masquerade costumes.

Statues and urns at regular intervals surmount the balustrades surrounding these gardens and add to the overall effect of architectural richness, as do gate piers crowned by figures of Perseus, beyond which lead the paths and driveways of the ornamental woodland. By the late 18th century these gardens were attracting many visitors, all of whom were enchanted, including the Englishman William Beckford, who described his meeting with the royal Infanta, Carlota Joaquina.

"Cascades and fountains were in full play: a thousand sportive *jets d'eau* were sprinkling the rich masses of bay and citron, and drawing forth all their odours, as well-taught water

OPPOSITE
A view across the main parterre in the Garden of Neptune reveals the balance achieved between the planted urns and enclosing balustrades and the pattern of hedged flowerbeds and paths.

BELOW
A section of the glorious painted-tile decoration of the canal that is Queluz's unique and most exhilarating feature. This is where members of the court took boat rides serenaded by an orchestra.

is certain to do on all such occasions! Among the thickets, some of which received a tender light from tapers placed low on the ground under frosted glasses, the Infanta's nymph-like attendants, all thinly clad after the example of Royal and nimble self, were glancing to and fro, one instant and invisible at the end." Then, in an amphitheatre in the heart of the formal woodland, Beckford continued: "I beheld the Alcina of the place, surrounded by thirty or forty young women every one far superior in loveliness of feature and fascination of smile to their august mistress."

The exotic atmosphere of the gardens that Beckford was able to enjoy himself was more often given over to larger gatherings of the court of the royal family. Aviaries of rare birds and a menagerie of wild animals were among the attractions, but the most popular entertainment was a boat ride along an elaborate tiled canal. Formed by damming a stream, this canal's inner walls of blue-and-white tiles made by João Nunes were decorated with maritime scenes and its outer ones lined with polychrome ceramic tiles with rural scenes, some of which were ordered from Mañuel da Costa Rosado. On a bridge spanning this canal stood a music room, in which an orchestra provided music for the gondolas floating underneath. Sadly, the music room collapsed, but when the canal was restored in the late 19th century it was replaced with a copy of Giambologna's statue *The Rape of the Sabine Women*.

At Queluz the display techniques of other royal gardens in Europe laid out for the entertainment of courts and visitors with formal parterres and classical-style statuary were used but the tiled decoration of the canal and other features made it uniquely Portuguese and transformed the overall character of the gardens. As the discerning 20th-century English designer Russell Page wrote after visiting Queluz: "Built when the extravagances of the Braganza kings were astonishing Europe, this canal with its exuberance of shape and colour, expresses all that is best in Portuguese gardens."

Peterhof

ST PETERSBURG · RUSSIA

I t is hard to think of any other garden in Europe more driven by the desire to compete with other royal examples and celebrate royal authority than Peter the Great's garden at Peterhof. The palaces and gardens that were built and laid out during his reign spearheaded the energetic tsar's campaign to westernize Russia. Introducing European culture to his country was, he believed, the best way to drag it out of the insular medievalism that the country's enormous size had encouraged for centuries. And there were no stronger visible demonstrations of European influence than grand classical palaces and lavish ornamental gardens.

Peterhof was the most symbolic of all Peter's efforts. Positioned some 30km (18 miles) west of St Petersburg, on the Gulf of Finland, it was begun in 1714, by which time Russia's victory in the Great Northern War against Sweden was looking assured. Just over a decade earlier the tsar had begun the creation of St Petersburg, his great city that would rise from the marshy estuary of the River Neva to announce his challenge to Sweden as the main Baltic power. The creation of Peterhof would celebrate Russian achievement and present a clear indication of its new-found European sophistication.

RIGHT
The view from the marble staircase of the central cascade across fountain pools to the elegant garden house, Marly. In the far distance the sea forms the horizon, as Peter the Great had always intended.

BELOW
"Peterhoff. Maison de plaisance de Sa Majesté Imperiale…" An etching, contemporary colour by Niquet c.1784, after a drawing by Louis Nicolas Lespinasse, showing the exhilarating scale of the gardens and palace.

Combined with his desire to celebrate military success was Peter's determination to compete with what he had seen during successive stays in Europe in 1697, 1712, and 1717. Despite spending much time in the Netherlands, mainly to study Dutch boat-building and the Dutch navy at first hand, it was not to Dutch gardens that he turned for his model. There was only one real garden example that Peterhof emulated and that was Versailles, the grandest in Europe. As Versailles was symbolic of Louis XIV's absolute monarchy, so Peterhof would present Peter the Great as Russia's ruler.

Two years after the work at Peterhof began Peter made his intentions quite clear (and at the same time demonstrated the power of royal patronage) when he made Jean-Baptiste Le Blond his Architect General, giving him the authority over all his palace and garden projects. Le Blond was arguably the most brilliant pupil of André Le Nôtre, Louis XIV's garden designer at Versailles. Le Blond survived for only three years after his arrival in Russia, dying in 1719, after which his work was continued by Niccolò Miccetti. But his influence on the gardens was huge, and he was responsible for the favourable comparisons to Versailles that were forthcoming from many visitors, including the German writer Christian Hirschfeld: "The largest and most splendid pleasure garden which Peter the Great had developed, though in the old formal manner, is

undoubtedly the garden at the palace of Peterhof....This garden deserves to be named the Russian Versailles, by analogy with its precious and manifold buildings, the fountains, cascades, marble motifs in the gardens that are termed game reserves; in certain respects this garden has many advantages as compared to Louis XIV's sumptuous garden."

Le Blond was well aware that he was expected to produce a garden that combined magnificence with drama. Peter wanted it to be grand but he also wanted excitement. Le Blond had the enormous advantage of the topography; the palace was built on a natural terrace from which the ground dropped away sharply to the north before levelling out gently towards the Gulf of Finland. Given the significance of the sea to Peter in his battles against Sweden and because, for him, it provided the symbolic link to Europe for Russia, the Peterhof garden was always going to be developed primarily in this direction. The steep terrace allowed for a combination of deep grottoes and marble cascades, with an array of statuary and fountains on descending levels to give the garden a sense of exhilaration. Whereas in the cascades and pools immediately below the palace the atmosphere created by the fountains is one of exuberance, in the long central axis of the lower

ABOVE
The central Samson Fountain at the foot of the main cascade displays a scene of rich ornament and exuberance rarely equalled in any other garden. It is an embodiment of Peter the Great's ambition.

RIGHT
The long canal from the cascade and Samson Fountain to the sea symbolizes the achievement of Russia's victories, which secured access to the Baltic.

garden, where the water flows inexorably to the sea through a canal, the rows of fountains on either side only add to the picture of unbroken symmetry. This contrast is one of Peterhof's most lasting qualities.

As with the great water gardens of the Italian Renaissance, one of the key figures in the development of Peterhof was the hydraulic engineer, Vasily Tuvolkov, who worked out a supply system to keep more than 170 fountains on the go. The water was brought via a specially constructed canal from the hills over 20km (12 miles) away near Ropsha. To ensure sufficient supply he also devised the system whereby the basins in the upper park, to the south of the house, served as reservoirs for the fountains in the gardens to the north. With the necessary engineering assured, Le Blond was responsible for the exhilarating central design, whereby the water is channelled under the palace to emerge and pour down the marble steps of the cascade beneath the north façade.

Peter's affection for Europe is best demonstrated in the lower park, the areas on either side of the central canal with a series of *bosquets* linked by *allées* and decorated with a further array of fountains – some of them joke fountains to soak the unwary in a way that would have definitely appealed to the tsar's sense of humour – and especially in the three garden buildings Monplaisir, Marly, and the Hermitage, which were built by Le Blond and his predecessor, J.F. Braunstein. Monplaisir is in the style of a Dutch house and, like the Hermitage which has a moat and drawbridge, is positioned close to the sea, while the elegant Marly is surrounded by formal fishponds.

The extensive upper park on the far south side of the palace, laid out in a grandiose display of ornamental formal parterres, only serves to increase the effect of Peterhof's size. It also contains one decorative feature that aptly illustrates Peter's determination to Europeanize the Russian people.

OPPOSITE
*On either side of
the central canal are the
areas of the lower park
where shady tree- and
hedge-lined paths lead to
fountain basins and pools.*

LEFT
*A number of the
fountains are ingeniously
decorative, such as this
one where jets of water
spout in an umbrella
shape from a gilded ball.*

Each statue in a group illustrating Aesop's fables is clearly labelled showing who they were and giving the message of their story so that Peter could be sure that Russian visitors understood and learnt the moral of the tales.

As at Versailles, the statuary at Peterhof is fundamental to the garden's overall appearance and the stories behind the picture. The connection with Louis's garden continued beyond Le Blond, when the craftsmanship of the Peterhof statues was overseen by Nicolas Pineau, a pupil of Antoine Coysevox, who had worked at Versailles. But the overriding impression – and, indeed, the one Peter the Great intended – is of vitality and victory, encapsulated in the water pouring from the cascade into the main central basin and its memorable sculpture group of Samson and the Lion as its centrepiece. Samson has forced open the jaws of the lion that

is about to expire, and the scene celebrates Peter's victory over Charles XII of Sweden at the Battle of Poltava. This powerful message combined with the brilliance of the gilded statues, marble steps, and cascade presents the visitor with as strong a display as to be found in any other garden in Europe. It is to the eternal credit of the Russians that, as with the other great palaces and parks around St Petersburg, painstaking restoration has been carried out on Peterhof since it was damaged during World War II. From that moment the garden has pulsed with the glittering vitality of its original creation and has integrated modern mechanics into the waterworks. It renews the reminder of Peter the Great's original ambition to show that he could make a garden in the European mould, which means it does not have the distinctive, more pastoral atmosphere of other royal Russian gardens.

LEFT
To one side of the spectacular central axis Palazzo Reale was given Italy's first giardino inglese *in the 1780s, on the advice of Sir William Hamilton, the British ambassador to Naples.*

RIGHT
In the first of the memorable sculpture groups that adorn the descending cascade, Diana and her nymphs are disturbed by Actaeon on the far side of the water.

Palazzo Reale

CASERTA · ITALY

The concept of display in royal European gardens and the influence of Versailles were carried to an extreme in the mid-18th century at Palazzo Reale, by Louis XIV's great-grandson, Charles III, the Spanish King of Naples. His father, Philip V, had created the gardens of La Granja at Segovia in Spain, where the dominant feature is the cascade, but on this dramatic site outside Naples his son went to altogether more dramatic lengths. As with the gardens of Peterhof, Nymphenburg, and Versailles there was an element of celebration of victory in their creation; Charles III had recently succeeded in recapturing the Kingdom of Sicily and Naples from Austria during the Polish War of Succession. A further incentive, no doubt, was to emulate the Renaissance gardens of his mother's Italian family, the Farneses.

In 1752 Charles commissioned the Neopolitan architect, Luigi Vanvitelli to design the grandiose palace and surrounding gardens. After Vanvitelli's death in 1773 the work was continued by his son, Carlo. In one direction the palace faces towards Naples, but the central garden feature was created on the other side, stretching up along a vast axis right into the wooded hillside, and dominated by water descending in a series of cascades and canals. The scale is stupendous – the

OPPOSITE
Water pours over the central wall into the Juno Basin, where the goddess and her attendants confront Aeolus. The balustrade is decorated with shackled figures representing the slaves who built the garden.

BELOW
A view up the central canal that leads to the palace showing the enormity of the design stretching through successive fountain basins to the cascade cut into the wooded hillside.

water flows from a point on the hillside 3km (2 miles) from the palace and in one section, the main cascade, it tumbles over enormous stone blocks for a distance of 78m (255ft) into the first of a series of basins decorated with figures from Classical mythology. In this basin the hunter Actaeon discovers Diana bathing with her nymphs and from here the water disappears underground to re-emerge in another basin with a fountain of Venus. From here it flows down the wide steps of a more gentle cascade and, once again, disappears below ground to reappear in the Ceres Basin before going down a further cascade or water-staircase into a basin decorated with the scene of Juno confronting Aeolus.

Everything about the gardens had a monumental element, and the clear intention was a daring display of ingenuity imposed on a dramatic natural landscape. The demands of the water system were only met by a supply from Monte Taburan over 40km (25 miles) away and brought by means of an aqueduct that in one place crosses the Maddalone valley via a huge triple-arched bridge. Slave labour was used to hack away the hillside for the foundations of the main cascade, and their figures are immortalized in the statuary of the Juno Basin; contorted figures shackled together in pairs surmount the balustrade overlooking the pool.

In the end the size and cost meant that the gardens were never completed to Vanvitelli's original designs, which included channelling the water under the palace and into two canals to flank the Via Appia for 20km (12 miles) to Naples. Unfinished or not, Palazzo Reale remains a uniquely theatrical display, a monument to royal ambition at the height of the complex series of dynastic struggles between Europe's intertwined royal families.

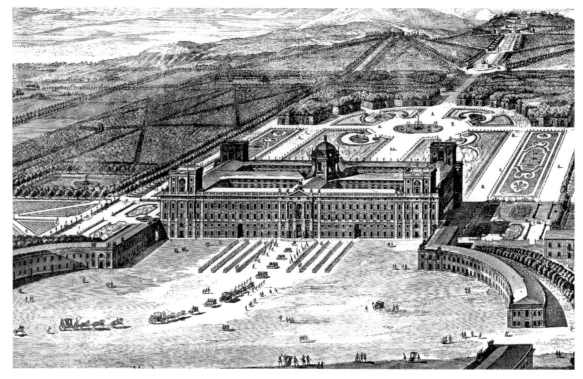

RIGHT
A contemporary engraving showing the grand piazza on the side of the palace facing Naples and the design for the main gardens that was never fully executed.

THE AGE
OF LEISURE

FOR MANY ROYAL GARDENERS the most important aspect of their gardens has been the provision of pleasure – creating places for relaxation, however impressive the surroundings. In many countries some of the rigid formalities of social life began to relax during the 18th century, and this was reflected in attitudes to gardens. It became less important for a garden to make a statement than for its ability to provide an atmosphere of enjoyment. This was particularly evident in the rococo gardens in Germany that delighted a series of the monarchs who created them in the different states and has been highlighted by the garden historian Ursula Grafin zu Donha: "The gardens attached to princely residences no longer had a merely representative function but served to promote social intimacy: they were divided into numerous small garden rooms, usually enclosed by hedges, gazebos, or trellises. There is something deliberately confusing, sometimes even labyrinthine in the layout of these gardens."

In some places, such as Drottningholm in Sweden, the new mood was introduced to an existing garden. Here the superb baroque layout created at the end of the 17th century was retained, including its memorable ornamental features of which the Hercules fountain statue group (*see pp. 40–1*) by

Adrien de Vries was the most notable. But by the middle of the 18th century the king's wife, Queen Louisa Ulrika, had different priorities and made new additions of her own that transformed the garden's mood, in particular the colony of Chinese houses and other decorative buildings in an area of the park that was called Kina, or China. Her gardening aspirations were driven by aesthetic desires that reflected the changing philosophy of the time, the influence of the Enlightenment, and the philosopher Rousseau, which together encouraged a more contemplative, leisurely enjoyment of gardening.

Influences such as these were definitely foremost in the gardening priorities of Queen Louisa Ulrika's brother, Frederick the Great of Prussia, as he demonstrated in his delightful garden at Sanssouci (*see below*). At first view, as parts of Drottningholm, the garden displays the formality and architectural ornament of the baroque age, but on closer inspection it is quite different – not least because of what Frederick sought from it. Although much of his reign was spent in military campaigns, his garden was in no sense designed as a triumphant illustration of his strength and success; rather the opposite. It was the place that provided undisturbed peace and enjoyment in a manner recommended by Voltaire, the philosopher and author so admired by Frederick. The emperor's approach to his garden was shared by his military and political enemy, Empress Maria Theresa of Austria, as demonstrated in the alterations that she carried out to the garden of Schönbrunn (*see opposite*).

The mood of enjoyment was already set in gardens that were attached to palaces serving as summer residences, notably Schwetzingen in Germany and Aranjuez in Spain. Designed as an escape from the rigours of city and court life they were, by definition, gardens of leisure regardless of the grandeur of much of their layout and decoration. In these places and others, the sense that they were open for a few weeks or months in the summer and then closed while no-one was in residence added considerably to the excitement of visiting them.

In some cases the palaces and their gardens were created in an earlier period, when the element of display was important. But they came into their own during ownership in the 18th century, when the provision of leisure and enjoyment was paramount, as was certainly the case at Schönbrunn and Schwetzingen. This led to the gardens taking on additional features, such as pavilions and other buildings set in the landscape for a particular purpose, which contributed greatly to the garden's atmosphere. Good examples were the Pagoda at Aranjuez, Maria Theresa's Menagerie at Schönbrunn, and Queen Louise Ulrika's village called China at Drottningholm. Some people would have called such features eccentricities, but they were quite acceptable in an atmosphere of enjoyment and were representative of not only a period but a style of gardening that in some cases continued into subsequent eras.

In a number of the gardens their royal owners did some gardening themselves for their own pleasure and relaxation. Frederick the Great tended his fruit and vines, his sister delighted in her flower garden, and the same was to be true of gardens developed later, for instance Queen Victoria and Prince Albert's garden at Osborne House (see pp. 122–5).

For future generations the priorities changed, as the enjoyment of leisure became overtaken by a desire for privacy. Until this happened, however, gardens created on an ambitious scale with ornate decoration and an array of architectural features were created by royal garden enthusiasts both for their own pleasure and the delight of their visitors. Where it involved adding something new to an existing garden, it almost invariably gave the garden a broader and more interesting appearance than if the garden had been restored and its original features replaced.

OPPOSITE
The low elegant façade of Sanssouci, Germany, faces the formal garden – a source of constant pleasure and relaxation to its creator, Frederick the Great.

ABOVE
Delightful patterns of flowers combine with the rich decoration of pavilions and other garden buildings in one spacious area of Schönbrunn, Austria.

PREVIOUS PAGES
The most impressive fountain basin at Drottningholm, Sweden, is topped by the figure of Hercules and celebrates the baroque inspiration for the original garden.

Aranjuez

ARANJUEZ · SPAIN

The fact that Aranjuez was developed in the 16th century by Philip II of Spain, specifically as a summer residence to escape from Madrid, set the tone for the gardens that he originally created but which were considerably expanded during the 18th century. Philip transformed what had been a hunting lodge into a palace and surrounded it with gardens that intriguingly combined the old Moorish influence that had previously dominated Spanish gardens, with the new influence from Holland and Flanders. Incidentally, Philip was brought up in the Spanish Netherlands.

Philip II planted English elm trees after admiring them on a visit to his wife, Mary Tudor, but his greatest legacy at Aranjuez was to create an island in the River Tagus. This island became the Jardín de la Isla, whose original appearance was applauded by a 17th-century English visitor, Lady Fanshawe, the wife of Charles II's ambassador to the Spanish court. "We went privately to see Aranjuez, which was most part of it built by Philip the Second, husband to Queen Mary of England. There are the highest trees, and grow up the evenest, that ever I saw; many of them are bored through with pipes for water to ascend and to fall from the top down one side against another, and likewise there are many fountains in the side of this walk, and the longest walks of elms I ever saw in my life. The park is well stored with English oaks and elms and deer; and the Tagus makes an island. The gardens are vastly large, with the most fountains and the best that ever I saw in my life." Lady

OPPOSITE
Aranjuez combines the exotic with the formal, as shown here with the medley of palms, pines, and other trees to one side of the hedged parterre.

BELOW
An engraving of the Treillage Gallery, one of the Aranjuez's most celebrated features in the 18th century.

Fanshawe visited at a time when the fountains were the gardens' most lively feature, not least the numerous trick ones that suddenly came into play along a path known as Los Burladores (the jokers).

Philip II's 16th-century palace was burnt down and it was the decision of Philip V to rebuild it during the 18th century and to rejuvenate the neglected gardens that brought a second period of glory to Aranjuez. Interestingly the work was supervised by two generations of a family of French gardeners, Esteban Boutolou, father and son, who not only carried out all the new designs but developed the garden by growing exotic species, which were mainly housed in a new conservatory. Their work built on Aranjuez's distinguished horticultural tradition, for in the 16th century it was the site of Spain's first botanic garden, established by Philip II; the tradition continues today in the superb vegetable garden, which takes full advantage of the fertile conditions.

In front of the palace a new parterre was laid out around the fountain of Hercules, a 17th-century addition. From the parterre Philip V's redevelopment spread out to the Jardín de la Isla, reached by a second stone bridge to add to the original one, and the island garden was revived with new avenues of limes, planes, and other trees, and smaller paths lined with hornbeam or evergreen hedges. The dominance of water over the garden was retained; in fact if anything it was enhanced as the presence of the river flowing past on both sides was maximized by the ingenious way the avenues and vistas were planned and in the development of the network of fountains and other architectural ornaments to which all paths led. Among the gardens' most intriguing elements are the groups of columns, usually surmounted with winged birds, which are

RIGHT
The formal network of tree-lined paths meeting at a series of fountain basins adorned by marble statues and with marble benches for relaxing is one of the garden's major features.

BELOW
The relationship between the garden and the river, in areas canalized to be incorporated in the design, is central to Aranjuez's atmosphere and appeal.

incorporated into fountain designs with the birds spouting water into a basin below. The air of enchantment that Philip II had originally created was revived, as confirmed by one visitor, Giuseppi Baretti, who visited Aranjuez in 1776: "A poet would say that Venus and Love had here consulted with Catullus and Petrarch to construct a country-residence worthy of Psyche, of Lesbia, of Laura – or some Infanta of Spain."

The atmosphere of pleasure was extended into a new area, the Jardín del Príncipe, by Philip V's successor, his son Ferdinand VI. This was a formal woodland garden designed to take full advantage of its position overlooking the River Tagus, not least with the broad walk known as the Calle de le Reina. Avenue-shaded paths led to more fountains and ornamental buildings, including a mock-cottage, which Marie Louise Gothein, the early 20th-century garden historian, described: "The little summer-house at the end of the garden, the Casa del Labrador, conceals under a modest name a luxurious park house." Most decorative of all the buildings are a pagoda and rotunda temple, both sited on small islands in a lake.

A riverside pier built during this period gave easy access for parties to go boating and enjoy the gardens in a leisurely way. It is not hard to imagine the Bourbon royal family and members of their court relaxing in the heat of the Spanish summer, for which the gardens provided a cool antidote and also a suitably exotic spectacle. The mixture of lush foliage, plentiful water, and flamboyant architecture was the pre-eminent quality during the 18th century, and it remains the same for visitors today. And to balance the elements of grand formality such as the parterre and Calle de le Reina along the river, the ecelctic mixture in the ornaments and the elements of surprise in the Jardín del Príncipe provide a reminder that this was a garden made for enjoyment rather than prestige.

At the same time the ramshackle village of Aranjuez, the home of the Spanish court when the royal family were in residence at the palace, was incorporated into the design with a new symmetrical layout of streets, some of which linked up with avenues radiating out from the garden. Not surprisingly, the residents were proud of the place, as described by the Englishman H.V. Morton after he visited early in the 20th century. "Castilians who have never travelled believe that Aranjuez is the lushest spot on this planet and a faithful replica of the earthly paradise. It is, in effect, a little corner of France beside the Tagus. Here the Bourbons erected a palace in imitation of Versailles, with grottoes and fountains, with endless avenues and shady places, where it seems that the music of the last fête champêtre has only just died away."

RIGHT
Two delightful garden buildings in the Jardín del Príncipe, the pagoda and domed rotunda, both on their own small islands in a lake.

Sanssouci

POTSDAM · GERMANY

The literal translation of *sans souci*, "without wordly cares", encapsulates what the Prussian king, Frederick II (Frederick the Great) aspired to when he decided to expand on the site of his father's original ornamental kitchen garden and built the long, low palace to which he would retire for peace and relaxation. It was here he came between his military campaigns against Empress Maria Theresa of Austria, to enjoy his paintings by Jean-Antoine Watteau, to write, to play the flute, and to converse with a select group of enlightened visitors who occasionally included Voltaire, with whom he corresponded for years. While Louis XIV had gardened for grand effect, half a century later Frederick did it for enjoyment and continually romanticized the pastime, for instance in his constant references to the merits of gardening as expounded by Virgil in *Georgics*. "I read Virgil's *Georgics* in the morning. I send my gardener to the devil for he says neither Virgil not I know anything about gardening." Even when entertaining he made sure he maintained his privacy, as his guests stayed in a separate pavilion especially designed for them.

RIGHT
A picture of serene symmetry, looking from the lower parterre across the series of terraces used for fruit and vine growing to the long, low façade of the palace complementing the garden's design.

BELOW
A detail of the garden's most exotic ornament, the Chinese Tea House, showing gilded Chinese figures around two of the supporting columns, which were fashioned like trunks of palm trees.

RIGHT
*The balance of foliage
and ornamental statuary
and light and shade, and
the continual lure of vistas
through the garden, is
well illustrated here.*

RIGHT
This copper engraving, dated 1748, coloured by Johann David Schleuen the Elder, shows a contemporary "view of the Royal retreat of Sans-Souci near Potsdam", during the first phase of the palace's development.

BELOW
An aerial view showing the ensemble of palace, terraces, and lower pool, and the superb regularity of the design, as well as the curious curving lines of the terraces.

As well as enjoying the ornamental aspect of gardening Frederick was particularly enthusiastic about the practical side. From cultivating his own fruit he moved on to develop the most prominent feature of his garden at Sanssouci, the series of six terraces descending from the palace, shaped in parabolic curves to maximize the sun's warmth. Here he planted vines against the retaining walls of the terraces, and along each of these 28 pairs of glazed windows were added to protect the vines in winter. As well as the vines the walls supported peaches and other tender fruit trees that gave the garden the productivity that Frederick so enjoyed.

Below the terraces a parterre was laid out originally in a pattern of eight *broderie* beds and centring on a large pool and fountain. The pattern of the parterre has been simplified, but the basin and fountain retain their important statues illustrating the story of the sea-nymph Thetis. The group includes figures of Air and Water sculpted by François-Gaspard Adam and Mercury and Venus by another Frenchman, Jean-Baptiste Pigalle, and given to Frederick by Louis XV. As if to emphasize the domestic, not grandiose, inspiration for the garden, the central vista from the vine terraces through the middle of the parterre and Thetis Fountain continued on to end not in some striking ornament but a gardener's cottage.

The garden developed mainly on both sides of the terraces; to the east a hothouse was replaced by a picture gallery designed by J.C. Buring (who took over from Frederick's original architect, Georg-Wenzeslas von Knobelsdorff after the latter's death), with a terraced garden descending below. The more important area of development was to the west, especially after Frederick's decision to build the Neues Palais (designed by Buring) to accommodate his guests. It lies at a distance of 2km (1¼ miles) from the main palace and is approached by an avenue off which different areas of the garden were created in the style of an ornamental park. Von Knobelsdorff had already built the Obelisk Portal, the Neptune Grotto, and the Marble Colonnade – the last in the style of the colonnade in one of the *bosquets* at Versailles but demolished towards the end of the 18th century – before Buring added Sanssouci's most audacious and eccentric ornament, the Chinese Tea House.

Writing in the early 20th century Marie Louise Gothein criticized it as "one of the most freakish attempts in this foreign style". She continues in a more charitable tone, however: "The cheerful little rotunda has an overhanging roof with a Chinaman on the top, supported on gilded palm-trunks; round the columns are grouped Chinese figures taking tea. The whole place is merely a fancy, and it lies prettily in the middle of a space bordered with hedges, which opens on three of its sides into small grass paths, narrowing as they advance." The tea house may have attracted much ridicule from purists,

but its detail is undeniably engaging, and when the sun catches the gilded parasol shading the Chinaman perched on the circular roof, it is an arresting sight.

During the early 19th century Frederick William IV, whose grandfather had succeeded the childless Frederick the Great as his nephew, created the Charlottenhof Park, adjacent to Sanssouci. At the same time he redesigned the layout of much of the parkland with winding paths and new ornamental trees. The main garden buildings happily survived, however, as did the main sweep of Frederick's garden from his palace across the vine terraces to the parterre below. Perhaps because Frederick always used Sanssouci for his own pleasure, rather than for court entertainment, it has an intimate atmosphere to an extent that is rare among royal gardens of the 18th century. No visitor leaves without having cast their mind back to the warring but enlightened Prussian ruler who gained his greatest relaxation from his garden at Sanssouci.

Drottningholm

STOCKHOLM · SWEDEN

Perhaps because it was built for a queen, or because it stands on an island, the outstanding royal garden in Sweden has an air of secluded dignity that no visitor can fail to notice. Its name combines the two characteristics, *drottning* for "queen" and *holm* for "small island", and its creation came about following the death of King Charles X in 1660, when his widow Hedvig Eleonora decided she needed to retire from court life in Stockholm but have a home within easy reach of the city. She struck upon one of the islands in Lake Malaren to the west of the city (now in the suburbs), with an old, originally medieval, castle. When this burnt down in 1661 she commissioned the architect Nicodemus Tessin to build the present baroque palace around which she created a suitable formal garden.

Tessin produced a number of garden plans that survive, including one dated 1665 which the garden historian Gosta Adelsward has suggested to be too sophisticated for him (he trained as a fortifications engineer) and argues that instead "it was drawn up in France under the supervision of Le Nôtre." Le Nôtre's design would have been made all the more likely by the fact that Charles XI was fighting as the ally of Le Nôtre's patron, Louis XIV, at the same time that his mother was commissioning her new garden. In the event it

OPPOSITE
The tall limes of the central avenue frame the view back to the palace across the formal parterre gardens, a vista that celebrates the continuity of baroque gardens.

BELOW
A gateway with gilded decoration centring on the crown and royal cipher opens to one of the lime avenues that line the garden's formal walks.

would appear that the garden was actually produced from a plan of 1681 by Tessin's son – a design that incorporates many features of the earlier version.

The 1681 plan confirms the measurements of the formal garden, 800 x 180m (2,625 x 590ft), an area enclosed by double avenues of lime trees as originally planned. The relationship between the gardens and palace has always been presented to the best advantage because the palace is raised up on a terrace giving it a slight elevation. From the palace an elegant double flight of steps descends to an extensive parterre, the central block of the garden, where much of the original pattern has been simplified since restoration in recent decades, but its focal point is still a large basin and outstanding sculpture group of Hercules by the sculptor Adrien de Vries. This was removed from the Wallenstein Gardens in Prague after a Swedish victory, and most of the other equally fine statues and urns around the gardens were similarly taken from either Poland or from Denmark.

Below the main parterre lies the garden feature most obviously inspired by French baroque, the water parterre with eight circular or oval basins, each with fountains. This parterre and the oval basin and cascade wall, which lie to one side, underwent extensive restoration during the 1960s. Beyond the water parterre the original baroque garden extended into *bosquets* divided by a pattern of straight paths, where the formality has been to some extent naturalized.

ABOVE
Drottningholm's island position provides such idyllic pastoral scenes into which the edges of the garden are subtly integrated with ornamental touches, such as the wrought-iron bridge balustrade.

RIGHT
The pure shades of green in the main parterre give a simplicity to the design that enhances the formal combination of plants, fountains, and immaculately kept gravel pathways.

LEFT
*Queen Louisa Ulrika,
Frederick the Great's
sister, who developed
the gardens during the
18th century, would have
delighted in this tranquil
view along the water.*

RIGHT
*The palace's elevated
position on a raised
terrace increases the effect
of the memorable central
view across the garden's
successive formal areas.*

Part of Hedvig Eleonora's formal deer park, which enclosed both sides of the main area, was developed into a highly individual garden of its own by another Swedish queen for whom Drottningholm was also the favourite home, Louisa Ulrika, the sister of Frederick the Great. She created a miniature village called China and described by Marie Louise Gothein: "Round a plot of ground there were pretty little houses in the Chinese style, the chief one adorned with tables of lacquer and Chinese figures. There was a Chinese pagoda with a bell-tower, also Chinese vases in porcelain, and gilt statues." The cultivated queen and her husband, King Adolphus Frederick, made a lasting impression on an English visitor, A.L. Hamilton – something he recorded in 1763: "Their majesties, with a select entourage, made their way at noon most days to China, a little pleasure palace….The King worked at his lathe, the Queen listened to her reader…the Princesses made lace, Prince Karl sailed a frigate, Prince Frederick ran about in the fields, the guards smoked."

A larger area of the park was redesigned during the 1780s for their successors by Fredrik Magnus Piper, who laid out an English-style landscape park inspired by Stourhead, which he had recently visited. Today the palace and gardens are the official residence of the present King and Queen of Sweden, and while the formality of the original gardens is immaculately preserved in the main central block leading away from the palace, the surrounding areas with fine trees, glassy glades, and waterside walks provide the ideal complement. Throughout the garden there is an air of serenity that one feels has been a constant characteristic ever since its creation nearly 350 years ago, and has fortunately been undisturbed by the elements of restoration that are inevitable to maintain the standards of a formal garden of this age. The double avenues that frame the parterres are undergoing a steady programme of replanting, and similar attention has been paid to the statuary, ornamental gateways, and other architectural features.

First and foremost, Drottningholm is redolent of its creator, Queen Hedvig Eleonora. As a wise and much-loved old lady she was helpless to stop the warring instincts of her grandson that would lose the country its Continental lands. From that period for many people she represented a golden age for the country. Emanuel Swedenborg lamented this in a poem entitled: *Sapphic Ode to the Deceased Dowager Queen Hedwig Eleonora of Sweden,* written in her honour after her death.

Schönbrunn

VIENNA · AUSTRIA

Versailles was yet again the competitive inspiration for Austria's grandest royal garden, an opportunity for the Habsburg Holy Roman Emperor, Leopold I, to express the intense rivalry he felt towards Louis XIV and, as in the case of other great royal gardens of the period, celebrate military victory. The chosen site had a far more peaceful origin; in the mid–16th century the son of Emperor Ferdinand I, Maximilian II purchased an idyllic–sounding property with a mill and farm and lusciously fertile ground, which he turned into a private hunting reserve. When a spring was discovered on the property he ordered that the water be brought to the small garden he had made and gave the place its name, *schön brun*, meaning "beautiful spring". In 1682 the Turkish siege of Vienna shattered the peace, and the old house was destroyed. Five years after the siege was raised, Emperor Leopold ordered Fischer von Erlach to draw up plans for a palace and gardens that would rival Versailles. The scheme was certainly ambitious enough, as Geoffrey Jellicoe has described: "The first designs were prodigious. Von Erlach placed the palace on the rising

RIGHT ABOVE
A view across the formal garden in front of the palace reveals the degree to which the baroque architecture combines with the garden features for the overall effect.

RIGHT BELOW
An early plan of the garden showing how the existing woodland was brought into the formal scheme.

BELOW
The original decision to build the palace on the elevated position was abandoned, and only decades later was the view across the formal garden completed with the addition of the arched Gloriette.

land to the south with a great architectural garden and a cascade of seven streams leading towards the plains, with the distant city as a background."

In the event the scheme proved too ambitious and had to be modified, so the palace was positioned on an easier site, and the elevated original position was eventually taken by the best-known feature in the Schönbrunn landscape, the Gloriette. The main garden was laid out in a long, thin rectangle roughly the width of the new palace, stretching towards the rising ground, with woodland on both sides and extending up the hill, in an manner not dissimilar to the screens of woodland on either side of the main west garden at Versailles. The Frenchman Johann Trehet was responsible for many of the major projects. He was an engineer by trade and in 1695 he was dispatched to make a detailed study of French gardens and parks before starting work in 1698. He built the system of reservoirs, channels, and tanks that ensured the fountains would work; he ordered some 20,000 beech trees for the woodlands, and masses of yew trees for the parterres.

Originally the enormous parterre was laid out in an intricate *broderie* pattern, the sections divided by long paths and decorated with garden ornaments. Today, the style of planting follows that established in the 19th century, with seasonal bedding with clipped evergreens, although the broad outline, and in particular the sheer size of the formal gardens,

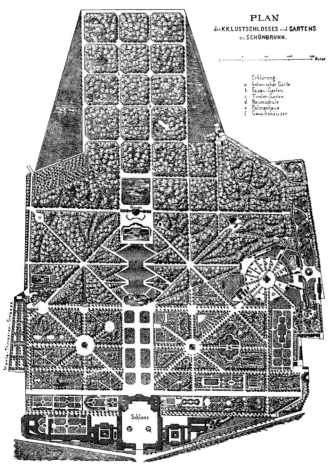

has hardly diminished. In von Erlach's original scheme much of the statuary celebrated the theme of the mighty Caesars and the all-powerful Habsburg dynasty. From the 1850s further statues were added portraying peaceful scenes from mythology.

Leopold's successor, Charles VI, paid little attention to the new palace, and it was not until his daughter, Maria Theresa, ascended to the throne in 1740 that work progressed. The heroic formality of the original scheme was toned down, in particular in the treatment of the wooded park, as the garden historian Paolo Morachiollo has described: "The concept of long straight paths and unlimited vistas, which seemed to lose themselves in the plain or forest, was set aside: hedges and trees were planted to create small enclosures which were shielded from the avenues running parallel or at right angles to the castle. These little enclaves…were full of surprises and discoveries: in one was a sculpture of Diana…in another the nymph of Schön Brun in her grotto…Maria Theresa's gardeners abandoned the unity of the original plan, with its vast sense of scale, heroic proportions and triumphal gestures, in favour of something better suited to a sober and enlightened monarchy which had no wish to perpetuate the cult of the individual sovereign but rather to magnify the importance of the monarch's official function."

RIGHT
These spectacular 19th-century glasshouses have been restored and filled with botanical rarities. Their size reflects the grandeur of the gardens overall.

BELOW
Decorative flowerbeds provide the link between the main formal gardens and the botanical gardens, in which exotic plants have grown for centuries.

In addition to these changes, the greatest visual impact from Maria Theresa's reign came from the construction of the Gloriette on top of the hill, where the palace was originally to have been built. The Menagerie that was designed to accommodate her husband Francis I's exotic birds was in the style of the one made at Versailles, and in the 1780s a composition of neo-classical ruins was erected as a focal point in the wooded park. This was inspired by the new picturesque taste in garden architecture that appeared in mid-18th century European gardens, either through the influence of German romanticism or through archaeological admiration of the Classical ruins in Italy.

Prior to its transformation into the site of a great palace the property of Schönbrunn had been renowned for its fertile land, so it was fitting that the growing tradition was continued with the establishment of a botanical garden, which remains to this day. Originally a Dutch garden growing a range of unusual exotics, it received its most impressive addition in the 19th century in the form of an enormous ornamental palm house that has now been restored and continues to add to the horticultural interest of the gardens. And while bringing a quite different element to Schönbrunn's original scheme, set with its own formal gardens in front to complement the architecture, it certainly remains faithful to the sense of scale that has always been a predominant feature.

During the 18th century the supreme illustrator of grand European palaces and gardens, the Italian artist Bernardo Bellotto (nephew and pupil of Canaletto) captured Schönbrunn in one of his most memorable views. While some of the period details he recorded have inevitably disappeared, the majestic scale of the whole ensemble remains inherent in the gardens today.

La Quinta del Duque de Arco

MADRID · SPAIN

OPPOSITE
The view down onto one of the two terraced parterres heightens the patterned effect of hedged flowerbeds and paths, and the symmetry of the design is matched by the architecture.

While the royal palace and gardens at Aranjuez lie some distance to the south of Madrid, a far more accessible haven has always been La Quinta del Duque de Arco, situated only some 15km (9 miles) from the city centre. It has been a summer retreat since the 15th century, and successive generations of the Spanish royal family have made alterations and additions to both the palace and its interiors, and the gardens. The gardens fell into disrepair, but by the early 20th century had been sympathetically restored, and while some of the original ornaments no longer decorate the terraces, others remain, and the patterned parterres have been replanted. Today the present King of Spain, Juan Carlos, entertains state visitors at the palace, and it is a frequently used residence. Much of the appeal of La Quinta derives from its spectacular setting in the park of El Pardo, which has large areas planted with vines and fruit orchards, giving it an overall appearance of productive beauty. The whole estate is concealed in a fold in the El Pardo hills and remains hidden to the unsuspecting visitor, until they arrive at the fine baroque stone gateway that dates from the 18th century and was built as the main entrance.

The original 15th-century palace was destroyed by fire in 1604 and rebuilt by Philip III. Less dynastically ambitious than his father, Philip's reign saw the end of wars against France, England, and the Netherlands that had been pursued by Philip II and witnessed a cultural zenith in Spain. In the early 18th century the estate was bought by the Duke del Arco, a close friend of Philip, who was ruling Spain at that time. A few years after the duke's death in 1737, his widow presented the estate to the king, and it has remained in royal ownership ever since.

Philip V was the first Bourbon king of Spain, and his accession sparked the War of Spanish Succession; as a result of this Spain's territorial power in Europe was severely reduced by the loss of the Spanish Netherlands, Sardinia, Milan, Naples, and Sicily. However, Philip's way of life in Spain was unaffected by the losses, and he poured money and attention on his palaces and their gardens and estates, including La Quinta and La Granja, in the mountains near Segovia.

Philip was strongly influenced by the Versailles gardens of his grandfather, Louis XIV, and by his powerful second wife, the Italian Elizabeth Farnese, who exerted political control for much of his reign. His work at La Quinta ushered in a long period of royal attention lavished on the estate, extending

through the next three reigns, and this was responsible for most of the palace's present appearance. He was succeeded first by Ferdinand VI, his son by his first wife Maria Louisa, and then by his younger son by Elizabeth Farnese, Charles III. In the palace and garden's 18th-century heyday it was visited by the well-known chronicler of Spanish life and artists, Antonio Ponz, who wrote: "Near the house there is a pretty garden, adorned with fountains, waterfalls, and numerous, rather ordinary marble statues. Choice fruit is gathered in the orchard and the Muscatel wine produced from the Quinta's vineyard is the most exquisite that can be found."

Each successive monarch, and subsequently Charles IV and his son Ferdinand VII, made alterations at La Quinta, but throughout it retained the French-inspired classical grandeur both in the architecture of the palace and the design of the gardens. These were laid out as intricate parterres on two large terraces, each focusing on a central pool and fountain. Successive architects worked for the different kings, including Carlier (whose son also worked at La Quinta), Esteban Marchand, Francisco Sabatini, and Mañuel de Molina. A detailed description of the gardens in 1840 is preserved in an inventory in the Madrid palace archives, and gives an idea of the garden's quality at that time: "Royal Quinta, first garden of the black fountain, divided into squares edged with semicircles of boxwood, rose bushes and other perennial plants. These four square beds are of very good design…all of the aforementioned

gardens are enclosed by iron railings with white stone pedestals at intervals, and good marble statues. Many of these railings have vines trained up them, enhancing their beauty. There are two fine avenues from the sides of this garden; one leads to the upper pond and the other down to the Madrid Gate. A large pool in the highest part is used to water the gardens with four water pipes bringing water from the Fuencarral side through conduits of brick and mortar. The water is sweet and good for drinking."

Positioned on a slight hill, the palace enjoys dramatic views over the surrounding countryside, and its elevation increases the visual impact of the terraced gardens situated below one façade, and laid out to maximize the impact of the natural incline. Of all the royal palaces La Quinta was the one particularly enjoyed by General Franco and it became his favourite residence throughout his time in power (1939–75). Both after wartime damage and, later, after a fire, extensive restoration was carried out on the palace and in more recent years the gardens have received similar attention.

One of the most distinctive features has always been the walls enclosing the two garden terraces with a symmetrical series of niches in which alternating urns and statues are displayed. Throughout, the gardens retain the strong sense of dominating architecture that was originally their primary objective, and the planting of the parterres conforms to the symmetrical requirements. Patterns of box hedging enclose the flowerbeds in groups and have the unusual feature of extra lines of hedging forming a series of decorative "borders" along the outsides of each of the groups. Busts also adorn the top of the retaining wall, flanked by a double flight of stone steps, and from its centre a cascade of water, perhaps the garden's most impressive feature, tumbles down to the lower level.

The overall design of the terraced parterres instantly gives the garden a wide horizontal spaciousness, and so the impact of the series of towering Wellingtonias on the terraces makes a dramatic contrast. These evergreen conifers were planted by King Amadeo during the 1870s and, while not part of the original parterre design, in the reconstruction they have been retained and add an impressive vertical element to an otherwise horizontal layout. And with the surrounding landscape clearly visible from the terraces the grandeur that was always intended to be La Quinta's most prominent characteristic has been retained from the 18th-century origins to this day.

The sense of remoteness that appealed to the original owners, and which certainly attracted General Franco, remains today, and the state visitors for whose use the palace is reserved have the sense of enjoying an oasis in an impressive but harsh landscape. For both palace and garden the air of well-ordered simplicity enhances the tranquil atmosphere.

OPPOSITE
Looking across one of the parterres to the distinctive enclosing wall with arched niches, containing busts and alternating with slender evergreens.

BELOW
There is striking contrast between the orderly parterres and their unusual pattern of double hedges, and the surrounding countryside visible beyond.

Schwetzingen

MANNHEIM · GERMANY

For centuries Schwetzingen, which lies close to the city of Mannheim, had been the summer residence of the Electors of Palatinate. The building was originally a moated medieval fortress but it was destroyed during the Thirty Years' War. In 1720, as a result of the successive wars, the Palatinate capital was transferred from Heidelberg, the centre of the German Renaissance, to Mannheim. Elector Karl Theodor came to power in 1743 and five years later he determined to rebuild the favoured home in a style that was not only better suited to the period than a medieval castle, but which, in its garden, produced one of the most original formal designs of any grand garden of the period. The primary influence was French, but the combined efforts of the architects and garden designer ensured that, within the restrictions of formality, the

OPPOSITE
Swirling patterns emphasize the curving lines of the circular parterre in front of the castle, and the symmetry is enhanced by the avenues of lime trees.

BELOW
The castle's elegant façade provides the centrepiece to the overall design, and the curving lines of the garden echo those of the architecture seen in one wing of the Zirkelhauser.

result would be a delightful move away from the regimented straight-lined symmetry so popular earlier in the 18th century. It was significant for the future that, in 1778, having succeeded as Elector of Bavaria, Elector Karl Theodor moved his court to Munich, and this, perhaps, limited the possibilities of later alterations to his gardens at Schwetzingen.

Theodor employed the architect Nicolas de Pigage, but he also engaged a renowned theatre-designer of the time, Galli da Bibiena, which may account for some of the originality. The new palace was flanked by two detached curved buildings, which together were called the Zirkelhauser. From this architectural framework the gardener to the Palatinate court, Johann Ludwig Petri produced a design. A coloured drawing dated 1753 of Petri's plan survives and was described by the garden historian Helmut Reinhardt: "The two circular buildings known as the 'Zirkelhauser' which were used as an orangery and banqueting rooms, project from both ends of the palace forming quadrants enclosing a semicircular parterre. The circle is completed by *berceux* which echo the Zirkelhauser: it

is then extended to form a square by the addition of spandrels, and is finally extended westwards to form a rectangle. This is without parallel in European garden design."

Petri's plan was implemented by Pigage. While the design of the garden was original within the confines of the formality of the age, its thematic arrangement and decoration also satisfied the requirements of the rococo style so popular in Germany at the time. The garden had a strong axial alignment through the centre of the circular parterre and at right angles, but as Reinhardt goes on to describe: "Yet in the new *bosquets* between these areas he [Pigage] created numerous intimate garden spaces connected with each other by a subtle *anglo-chinois* network of paths. These garden salons, which the Elector furnished with architecture, fountains, and sculpture, answered rococo society's need for diversion, variety, and refined play."

Much of the architecture and statuary echoes the originality of the overall design. One of the most prominent fountains is called the Stag Fountain with a white marble figure by the sculptor Peter Anton von Verschaffelt. Pigage designed the outdoor theatre, guarded by pairs of sphinxes with women's heads, where the celebrated court orchestra who were based in Mannheim performed. Aligned with the theatre and a delightful backdrop for audiences is the Temple of Apollo, a domed open rotunda. Pigage also designed Fountain of the Birds and the Bath House hidden away in the woods. The Fountain of the Birds shows in bronze the tale of an owl who killed another bird and as a punishment is constantly squirted with water by all the other birds of the world. The elector enjoyed entertaining his mistresses in the Bath House, where the lavishness of the marble interiors goes way beyond ordinary rococo decoration. And yet, in true rococo spirit, this was a garden intended not only to stimulate relaxation but also in which to find amusement and admiration in the imaginative variety of features incorporated into the overall scheme.

Many European royal gardens progressed from a formal original design to incorporate a later more natural style under successive owners, but at Schwetzingen for Theodor these changes came during his own lifetime and did not wait for his successors, as he instigated such alterations himself. In the late

OPPOSITE
The view from the theatre to Pigage's Temple of Apollo. The marble sphinxes are typical of the originality of much of the garden's statuary.

BELOW
The magnificent marble sculpture group of a hunted stag is one of the arrangements of ornaments along the vista from the splendid garden out into the surrounding countryside.

1770s he employed Friedrich Ludwig von Sckell, titled Court and Pleasure Gardener, to redesign the outer areas of the garden in the style of an English landscape garden. Continuity was retained, however, as Pigage designed the architectural ornaments for the new areas, including a Roman aqueduct, the Temple of Mercury, and the Turkish Mosque. The elector originally planned to sweep away all formal gardens, but von Sckell persuaded him to retain the main parterres and restrict the changes to the outer areas.

The most significant alteration to the landscape was to naturalize the formal lines of the main canal, which became known as Der See (the lake). This now forms a winding lake across the end of the gardens beyond the parterres and close by Pigage added two of his later buildings, the Temple of Mercury and what can be seen as Elector Karl Theodor's last great extravagance at Schwetzingen, the Turkish Mosque. Flanked by minarets the mosque looks over the lake in one direction; on the other side is a courtyard enclosed by colonnades.

At the time not everyone approved of the elector's changes. Christian Hirschfeld, who considered himself the undisputed arbiter of gardening taste in Germany in the late 18th century, visited in 1784 and criticized the mosque: "Look at the Mecca scene for example…this Mecca in the middle of the French part…this monument ought not, if the illusion is to be preserved, to be very different from ruins which are

RIGHT
The combination of water, plants, and ornament that make up the formal garden are well illustrated in this view along one of the enclosing canals.

BELOW
The Turkish Mosque illustrated in this engraving was built in the late 18th century and helped continue the established theme of enjoyment.

nearly worn away by the hand of time: but here everything is new, perfect, ornate." At about the same time the Englishman William Beckford visited and while he admired the formal gardens he dismissed the landscape: "I would fain have loitered an hour more, in this enchanted bower, had not the gardener, whose patience was quite exhausted dragged me away to a sunburnt contemptible hillock decorated with the title of *Jardin Anglais*. A glance was all I bestowed on this caricature upon English gardens."

The waspish Beckford was a seasoned traveller and often hard to please, but his comments also reflected an uneasy feeling among his contemporaries towards a garden that tried to combine contrasting styles from different periods and for whom the immaturity of the new landscape garden compared unfavourably with the established quality of the formal garden with its superlative statuary and water features. And, of course, Beckford was an Englishman who felt that the landscape style of gardening would never be executed to the same standards anywhere else in Europe as in his home country.

In time, however, the landscape garden has matured, and today one of the outstanding qualities of Schwetzingen is the coexistence of the formal and landscape gardens and the manner in which they are integrated by both paths and axes. The restoration brilliantly returned the exact symmetry that makes the parterre gardens so impressive, whether in the main circular area in front of the palace or in the rectangular area to one side, bounded on two sides by narrow canals and on a third by the long façade of the orangery building. The restoration also rediscovered the rich hues of the statues and other ornaments, the gilding of some figures such as Classical Atalanta or the brilliant white of the Germanic stags. In different directions the progression from French baroque formality to English inspired informality is presented with complete harmony, and while the whole ensemble may have been driven by the extravagance of the Elector Karl Theodor and his enjoyment of pleasure, the end result is a garden that in its restored state is a place where visitors combine enjoyment and admiration in equal measure.

ROYAL
LANDSCAPES

ENGLAND WAS ACKNOWLEDGED AS THE exclusive place of origin of the landscape garden by all gardeners in Europe who adapted the natural style in the 18th and 19th centuries. But it is an interesting fact that while a number of the outstanding landscape gardens created in Europe were royal gardens and are discussed in this chapter, the great English landscapes that they sought to emulate were not royal gardens but ones created by the land-owning Whig aristocrats who dominated English life during the 18th century.

Not all royal gardeners in Europe embraced this landscape style, or at least not immediately. In France, the entrenched tradition of the formal garden and, in some notable cases, the degree to which it had been simplified to become, in a sense, a formal landscape dependent upon water, trees, and open lawn focusing on a house or château, ensured that *le jardin anglais* was something of a rarity until the 19th century. Similarly, it hardly penetrated into Spain and Portugal, where decorative formality continued to dominate. In one unique instance, the Palazzo Reale at Caserta near Naples (*see pp.36-9*), an attempt was made to create a formal garden on such a massive scale that it took on the proportions of the surrounding landscape. The engraving of this garden on p.14 confirms the extent to which the interlinked series of formal water gardens marched inexorably up the hillside in the far distance, thereby bringing the landscape into the overall scheme. But the primary incentive for the garden was to create an enormous display, and for this reason it is discussed in the first chapter.

In some countries, however, royal gardeners were in the vanguard of taste and were even responsible for introducing the landscape garden to their country. The Russian empress Catherine the Great's enthusiasm for English culture manifested itself in the great art collection that she purchased from Sir Robert Walpole's heirs and the renowned service that

OPPOSITE
*An Arcadian scene of a
low arched bridge crossing
tree-lined water at Schloss
Dyck, Germany, in a
manner that typified
the interpretation of the
landscape movement
in Europe.*

RIGHT
*A view from the palace of
Wilanów, Poland, where
the roofscape is adorned
with classical statues that
match the formality of
the parterre below. Tall
trees around the edges
shroud the landscape
garden that lies beyond.*

PREVIOUS PAGES
*The Temple of Friendship
at Pavlovsk is one of
the most significant
expressions of the
landscape movement in
any garden in Europe.*

she commissioned from Josiah Wedgwood's porcelain factory. But it was equally apparent in the landscape garden she created at Tsarskoye Selo and the fact that she went to Britain for her architect and designer, Charles Cameron.

The landscape garden achieved remarkable maturity and style in a number of European royal gardens, fittingly nowhere more than Pavlovsk, the Russian garden that followed Tsarskoye Selo. Here Cameron's work continued for Catherine's son and daughter-in-law, and he produced a landscape that bears comparison with virtually any other on the Continent. While the English originals have the rarity of initiating the landscape garden, Pavlovsk emphatically demonstrates that the later European models were capable of achieving the same aesthetic goals. The combination of gardening and the natural landscape, the judicious positioning of garden buildings and their significance, often harking back to Classical overtones, and the creation of the landscape to focus on and revolve around the house (or, in this case, palace) were all true to the priorities of the English originals.

Other gardens discussed in this chapter, in particular Konopiste in Bohemia and Wilanów in Poland, illustrate the manner in which landscape gardens were often developed around an existing formal garden immediately in front of the house or palace. This was unusual in England; where a landscape garden was created with any real intent, it was not often that an existing formal garden was retained. Parterres were swept away, most famously in the work of "Capability" Brown. This did not happen in Europe and as a result many gardens have an enjoyable juxtaposition of styles. At Wilanów the terraced parterres in front of the palace lead to the landscape beyond, which gives the garden its most pleasant elements and mood. At Konopiste the gardens came much later, in the early 20th century, but again the combination was the same, with formal ornamental gardens leading to the spectacular wooded landscape on all sides.

At Tsarskoye Selo Catherine the Great paid the ultimate compliment to English gardens by commissioning an identical model of one of the most talismanic buildings of the movement, the Palladian Bridge at Wilton House in Wiltshire. Such admiration was even more evident in the garden at Wörlitz in Germany. Here Prince Franz of Anhalt-Dessau created the first landscape garden in Germany, and many of the buildings are directly modelled on originals found in English gardens, including a neoclassical temple, a Chinese bridge, and a Gothic house. It was, in a sense, similar to the derivative admiration that led earlier garden makers to faithfully reproduce certain features of Versailles and ensure that the Englishness of the landscape gardens was unmistakeable.

Tsarskoye Selo

ST PETERSBURG · RUSSIA

For many Russian intellectuals of the mid-18th century this was the place that encapsulated all their artistic and cultural aspirations. It was to inspire a host of famous poets, both contemporary and later in the 19th century, and they all agreed with Pushkin's opinion: "We are all the same: the whole world is foreign to us/Our fatherland is Tsarskoye Selo." During the Soviet period it was renamed Pushkin Palace in recognition of both the poet's reputation and the esteem in which Tsarskoye Selo was held. The estate lies 36km (22 miles) south of St Petersburg and it had been home to Peter the Great's wife, but it was transformed by Catherine the Great during her reign from 1762 to 1796.

Most importantly it was at Tsarskoye Selo that the English landscape garden was introduced to Russia, through Catherine's enthusiasm for English culture and the arts in general, and her specific admiration for English gardens. She wrote in a letter to Voltaire in 1772: "I adore English gardens, with their curved lines, *pente-douces*, ponds like lakes (archipelagos on dry land): and I despise deeply straight lines

ABOVE
The Ramp of the Cameron Gallery, *a watercolour by Semyon Shchedrin, dated 1794, showing the Cameron Gallery on the right and the* pente-douce *(sloping walkway) that rose on arches from the park.*

RIGHT
Looking across the lake to Cameron's architectural ensemble; the gallery with its swirling double staircase on the right and the façade of the palace behind on the left.

and identical *allées*. I hate fountains that torture water into running contrary to its nature…in a word, anglomania is more important to me than plantomania."

In the mid-18th century the Catherine Palace at Tsarskoye Selo was rebuilt in magnificent Russian baroque style by the architect Bartolomeo Rastrelli. At the time it was surrounded by an extensive formal park, large areas which Catherine was to recreate as a landscape park. For expert advice in the creation of her English-inspired garden Catherine turned to an English gardener, John Bush (who was born in Hanover and originally called Busch). Catherine dispatched one of her architects, Vasily Neyelov, to England to approach Bush, who, in 1771, sold his nursery in Hackney, London and left for Russia. After returning to England his son Joseph took over his gardening responsibilities for Catherine.

Bush was responsible for landscaping a large area of the New Garden at Tsarskoye Selo, and his name appears on a plan of 1780. He worked closely with Neyelov, who was responsible for many of the early buildings that adorned the

RIGHT
The Rostral Column and the Turkish Baths, two of the buildings that decorate the landscape in celebration of Catherine the Great's military victories.

BELOW
Even in the formal Old Garden views beyond the patterns of lawn and flowerbeds link it to the landscaped New Garden.

landscape including, most famously, the Siberian or Palladian Bridge that was modelled on Sir Roger Morris's original example in the gardens of Wilton House, Wiltshire, which Neyelov undoubtedly saw and studied when in England. Unlike the bridge at Wilton and the two others in England, at Stowe and Prior Park, Tsarskoye Selo's is unique in being built entirely of marble rather than more humble stone. The central feature of the new landscape was the Great Pond, an enormous naturally shaped lake that was created out of an existing formal basin with ambitious earthworks and engineering in the style of a "Capability" Brown landscape in England. Its naturalness was accentuated by pronounced bays and headlands sculpted along its edges, and it was linked to other smaller lakes by a complicated network of channels, some underground but others adorned with artificially created waterfalls, which the flat terrain did not allow to occur naturally.

After John Bush returned to England his work was continued by his son, Joseph while the Scottish architect Charles Cameron worked extensively on the palace interiors and many architectural features in the park. Most dramatic is the neoclassical Cameron Gallery, which he designed to enable Catherine to promenade and view both the old formal gardens on one side of the palace and the new landscape garden on the other. His imperial mistress clearly enjoyed it because when Cameron had completed the new building she paid him the enormous honour of naming it after him.

The splendid baroque Grotto built by Rastrelli afforded a view of the original formal basin and this was retained to overlook the naturalized Great Basin; however, Catherine added many other buildings and ornaments around the park, most with some allegorical meaning, and many celebrating Russian victories in the wars against the Turks. The Rostral Column that rises from the water beside a wooded island was designed by Antonio Rinaldi to celebrate the Sea Battle of Chesme, and another victory resulted in the Turkish Baths beside the lake – these were built in the form of a mosque complete with minaret. Catherine made it clear in writing that she was the chief enthusiast for celebrating the war in her new garden: "While this war continues, my garden at Tsarskoye Selo becomes more like a toy, after each glorious military action a suitable monument is erected in it. The Battle of Kagul…resulted in an obelisk with an inscription…the Sea

Battle of Chesme produced a Rostral Column in the middle of the Great Pond…moreover I have had the idea of having a Temple of Memory built in the little forest, the approach to which would be through Triumphal Gates where the previous actions in this current war will be represented in medallions."

If military victory gave rise to many of the ornaments in the new landscape exotic fantasy was behind others, most obviously seen in the Chinese-inspired buildings in the Chinese village. This was positioned on one side of the new landscape garden, adjoining the rectangular garden in front of the smaller Alexander Palace. Many of the buildings were designed by the architects Ivan Gerard and Yury Velten. Gerard and Neyelov designed the Great Caprice, an arched bridge surmounted with a Chinese open gazebo, which spanned one avenue. Velten designed the Creaking Pavilion, so named because of its deliberately creaking weather-vane.

Tsarskoye Selo introduced the landscape garden to Russia, and this in itself, in a country where the people's relationship with the natural landscape would grow to become enormously significant, was of major importance. At the time of its creation it fulfilled too many of Catherine's expectations to be able to claim any true purity of landscape, but once it had matured it arguably was of greater inspiration to Russian art and literature than any other garden.

LEFT
A view across the Great Pond that would do justice to any of the great English landscape gardens with the Hall in the foreground and the Palladian Bridge beyond.

ABOVE
The Palladian or Siberian Bridge designed by Neyelov surpasses its model that the architect studied at Wilton House, Wiltshire by being built entirely of marble.

Konopiste

PRAGUE · CZECH REPUBLIC

Originally built in the 14th century because of its strategic strength on a wooded hill on the main route from Vienna to Prague, the position of the Bohemian castle of Konopiste would later became the foundation for a romantic idyll. For centuries it was owned by a succession of leading Czech families, among whom the Vrtbas made the most significant impact. During the 18th century they transformed the old fortress by adding a new baroque entrance building from a new formal garden terrace – all designed by Franz Maximilian Kanka. The gardens were decorated with a series of neoclassical statues made by the outstanding Czech sculptor of the period, Mathias Bernhard Braun.

Konopiste's most significant period commenced over a century later, in 1893, when the estate was purchased by Archduke Franz Ferdinand, nephew and heir to the Habsburg Emperor, Franz Joseph. At odds with his uncle (who refused to acknowledge the nephew's marriage to a Czech countess),

RIGHT
The castle's picturesque turrets rise up above the gardens that surround it, and the elevated position provides memorable views across the landscape.

BELOW
This group of statues in one part of the garden typifies the ornamental quality achieved by Archduke Franz Ferdinand.

ABOVE
An aerial view confirms the castle's spectacular position overlooking the lake in one direction and the formal gardens on terraces below in another.

LEFT
The ornaments at Konopiste were added to by statues from Villa d'Este which Ferdinand inherited and positioned in the rose-filled, formal Italian Garden.

Ferdinand was always a stalwart supporter of the Czech and Bohemian cause within the Habsburg empire and Konopiste became a means to express this. After having remodelled the castle in a romantic neo-Gothic style, he lavished most of his attention on the gardens and park, which he created and which provided him with endless pleasure. To the south of the castle an enormous lake was dug and the park extended by 200ha (495 acres) and extensive woodlands planted, removing farmland in the process.

Ferdinand added his own outstanding inheritance to the distinguished ornaments he acquired when purchasing Konopiste. His mother was the sister of the last King of the Two Sicilies and it was through her that he inherited the collection of the Duke of Modena, which included the sculptures from Villa d'Este in Tivoli, Italy. They were used to decorate the series of new gardens commissioned by Ferdinand, in particular the Italian Garden, a formal rose garden created on the largest garden terrace. Thousands of roses were planted here – and all over the estate where they were used for hedges and Ferdinand also planted quantities of rare specimen trees. For him Konopiste was an expression of romantic landscape and a means of escape from a troubled life, which ended with his assassination in Sarajevo in 1914.

BELOW
From every vantage-point the formal patterns of the Italian Garden are backed by the surrounding wooded landscape into which paths lead in every direction.

Pavlovsk

ST PETERSBURG · RUSSIA

Tsarskoye Selo was the first essay in the English-inspired landscape garden in Russia and as such has a unique significance. The park at Pavlovsk, just a few kilometres away, however, was begun later, for Catherine the Great's son, Grand Duke Paul, and was to develop the Russian landscape garden onto a different plane, both intellectually and in scale. Given the enmity between Paul and his mother, whom he opposed at every opportunity, her gift of the estate to him to celebrate the birth of his first son to his second wife, Maria Fedorovna, was one of the rare instances of harmony between them. It was also Catherine's architect, Charles Cameron, who built and decorated the Palladian-inspired palace and carried out the first – and most important – phase of landscape work.

Throughout Cameron's time at Pavlovsk he was dictated to by the Grand Duchess Maria Fedorovna, a strong personality and keen gardener, who had been born Princess Sophia Dorothea in Württemberg, Germany. She was responsible for the initial English influence here, from her beloved homeland where her childhood gardens had quaint English buildings which she copied at Pavlovsk. Always a favoured home for the Grand Duchess, Pavlovsk became more important to her after the death of her parents and the assassination of her husband in 1801, five years after he had become tsar.

The park was huge and at the end of the 18th century it extended to over 1000ha (2500 acres). Within this vast area there were great differences of style and emphasis, all of which Cameron managed, from Marie Fedorovna's private flower gardens and whimsical decorations and buildings, such as her thatched dairy, to the vast tracts of forest into which geometric rides were cut to draw them into his overall plan. As a result, although Cameron was constantly required to make adjustments and the full extent of his landscape design was never finally completed, over a hundred years later the art historian Mikhail Alpatov wrote: "All of Pavlovsk in its entirety constitutes an enormous and integrated poetic world and not for nothing is one pillar on the edge of the park called 'the end of the world'."

Cameron ensured that the palace of Pavlovsk became the focal-point of all the elements within the new landscape, and the most important of these was the valley of the River Slavyanka, which wound its way through a variety of scenic terrains and provided the setting for a succession of landscape pictures. The garden historian Dimitri Shvidkovsky has described it as "one of the greatest achievements of landscape gardening in Russia". The changing natural scenery, from open valley with birch-wooded hills beyond to steep rocky

OPPOSITE
Looking across the River Slavyanka where it flows in front of the palace. The relationship between the valley and the building is one the great qualities of Pavlovsk.

cliffs or where the water widened out into an old mill-pond, was used as the basis of Cameron's landscape creation. Near the palace he made a lake to add a new natural dimension to the composition in which the palace was primarily integrated.

The buildings and architectural ornaments that Cameron designed for the landscape all had their own particular significance and were carefully integrated into the surroundings. As the garden historian Peter Hayden has described, the Apollo Colonnade emphasized the park's "role as a sanctuary" because Apollo was "the protector of valleys and groves and patron of the arts". This colonnade partially collapsed in the 19th century and is now a picturesque ruin. Without question the most imposing addition to the park was the building that still encapsulates Cameron's work at Pavlovsk, the Temple of Friendship. The chaste, domed, Doric rotunda stands on a peninsular beside the Slavyanka, and its gentle form blends with the native trees among which it nestles, just as Cameron intended in 1790. It was named in honour of a visit to Russia by Joseph II of Austria, son of the Empress Maria Theresa, who wrote to his mother after staying at Pavlovsk: "I was made to take part in laying the foundation stone of a temple, dedicated to Friendship, which I could not refuse." While the area around the Temple of Friendship

RIGHT
The Pier was one of the collection of picturesque buildings added to the landscape for the Grand Duchess Maria Fedorovna.

BELOW
A coloured engraving, 1801–3, by Komya Chesky of a view of the Pier in the garden of Pavlovsk, shortly after its completion, now held in the State Museum of Russia.

RIGHT
*A view up to the Apollo
Colonnade, which is
preserved as a semi-ruin
after a section collapsed.
It can be glimpsed at the
end of different vistas
through the landscape.*

OPPOSITE
*The White Birches,
an area added to the
gardens during
the 1820s to celebrate
northern Russia's
landscape of meadows
and birch trees.*

demonstrated Cameron's skill in integrating architecture to the landscape, in other areas his treatment relied entirely upon the natural features.

Among Cameron's final contributions to Pavlovsk were the Private Gardens, unsurprisingly, at the personal behest of Maria Fedorovna. Close to the palace he made a lavish formal garden, where masses of roses and other more exotic plants were complimented by statuary and which was overlooked by the Temple of the Three Graces in the form of an open, square, Ionic portico. But by the turn of the 19th century (by which time Paul had begun the brief reign that would end in his murder), the architect Vincenso Brenna made alterations to both the palace and the gardens. Andrei Voronikhin also made architectural additions in the form of garden structures and ornaments, including the Visconti Bridge and the centaurs on the bridge closest to the palace. As befitting the home of the tsar and his wife, the mood at Pavlovsk became more imperial during these years, but in the early 19th century Pietro Gonzaga introduced a pastoral naturalism with new changes, in particular the area known as White Birches, which was inspired by the meadow and forest landscapes of northern Russia and was far more in character with Cameron's work.

Like many other royal gardens and their palaces in Europe, Pavlovsk's character was heavily influenced by the succeeding events in the lives of its royal owners, and after the murder of Paul, when his widow the Dowager Empress remained, its reputation was tarnished along with that of the disgraced tsar. In a sense this feeling of melancholy only added to the atmosphere of the landscape, which few visitors have failed to be affected by, not least a succession of romantically inclined Russian authors and artists, including Pavel Svinin, who wrote in 1816: "If it is possible for art to approach nature, to replace it in all its games and appearances terrible and agreeable, magnificent and simple, then it is, of course, at Pavlovsk that it happens. These sullen cliffs, these roaring waterfalls, these velvet meadows and valleys, these dark mysterious forests seem to be original creations of graceful nature."

There was no greater compliment paid to Pavlovsk than the account by the English 19th-century gardening writer, John Claudius Loudon, that Pavlovsk was "the best park in the English style not only in the environs of the [Russian] capital, but also anywhere in the Empire" and the reason for this was because it had actually been designed by "Capability" Brown. Loudon maintained that Brown had received a description of the Slavyanka valley and had sent back a design: a completely apocryphal account, but one that confirms the reputation that the landscape had achieved within a few decades. Like the other palaces and gardens around St Petersburg, Pavlovsk has undergone extensive restoration since its devastation during World War II, but its wooded glades and valleys along the Slavyanka river and the various buildings continue to hold an atmosphere of melancholy beauty.

Wilanów

WARSAW · POLAND

Many royal gardens are entwined with the history of their nations, but none more so than Wilanów. In the 1670s a plot of land, then just outside the capital city of Warsaw, was transformed into one of Poland's most impressive palaces and gardens as the summer residence of Jan Sobieski, an aristocrat and military leader who had been elected to rule as King John III in 1674. But on his death, just over 20 years later in 1696, Poland effectively ceased to exist as an independent nation with a monarchy; indeed it did not regain its independence until the end of World War I in 1918 when it became a republic. In the interim period Poland was taken over by neighbouring countries.

At the time that John III came to the throne Poland was struggling to maintain its independence against powerful neighbours, including Austria, Prussia, Russia, Sweden, and, not least, the Ottoman Turks. In 1673 John's army defeated the Turks at the Battle of Khotin, and after becoming king he turned his attention to another constant national challenge – regaining territory that had been taken by Prussia. By the

RIGHT
A painting showing the main entrance of the palace and gardens at Wilanów during their heyday in the mid-18th century, by the master of such views, Bernardo Bellotto.

BELOW
The riches of the palace architecture and the parterre garden in front heighten the effect of the landscape garden that lies beyond.

1680s the Turks had regained military strength and in alliance with Hungary they attacked Vienna, the seat of the Holy Roman Emperor, Leopold I. John became a hero of all Christian Europe when he led the combined Polish and Imperial armies to first raise the siege of Vienna and then defeat the larger Turkish army.

Without doubt his prestige was highest during the early years of his reign, when he determined to make Wilanów a suitable summer residence. The palace was designed by the Dutch architect Tylman van Gameran, with a rich array of baroque flourishes such as the busts and life-size statues that line the roofscape. There are other intriguing decorative details, such as a moulded-plasterwork sundial on one wall, where the winged Chronos (the God of Time) tells both the time and the signs of the Zodiac, and similar effects were extended into the original gardens. These were created for John III by an Italian, Augustyn Locci, and a German, Adolf Boy, and were lavish French-baroque in a style that was most fashionable in Poland at the time.

Beyond the palace's courtyard the key features to survive are the upper and lower terraces and the *patte d'oie* (junction) of three radiating avenues in the style of Versailles that can also be seen at Hampton Court. Formal parterres were laid out on the terraces in a pattern integrating fountains and statuary to make one of the outstanding features of the garden. Fine figures adorn the stone balustrade along the top of the

retaining wall that divides the terraces, and attention is drawn to the group that decorates the staircase: they are representations of the four stages of love: Apprehension, Consummation, Boredom, and Separation. Another unusual feature is the *buffet d'eau* integrated into the retaining wall with a series of wall spouts emerging from stone panels into basins below. The rich, decorative ornament given to the *parterres de broderie* that originally graced the two terraces of the formal garden provided the link with the architecture of the palace and it confirmed that in Poland in the 18th century gardens were laid out to enhance a grand house or palace rather than to display their own individual qualities.

By the mid-18th century Poland had become a political pawn fought over by Prussia, Russia, and Austria with the first two controlling large areas of the original country. But a sense of nationality and independence still flourished and no doubt encouraged the introduction of the English-inspired natural landscape garden, which came with the work of Szymon Bogumil Zug, who suggested there was an aesthetic link between Poland's struggle to maintain her national identity and the romantic naturalism of the English landscape style. He moved to Poland from nearby Saxony in 1756, and his first Polish garden was designed in the 1770s for a relation of the king, Stanislaw August Poniatowski. Thereafter, he was responsible for the leading Polish gardens at the time and Wilanów, now belonging to another powerful aristocratic family, the Lubomirskis, followed the fashion. At this stage in the garden's history the position beside the River Vistula was capitalized to full advantage, and the new landscape garden was made beyond the original terraces, and given a sense of integration by the survival of the *patte d'oie*. At one point the river was expanded to form the curving lake, and water became a central feature of the new design.

The romantic theme was extended further in the early 19th century, by which time Wilanów belonged to the Potocki family. But a century later, like vistually every other great house and garden in Poland, Wilanów was devastated by the events of World War II. Fortunately during the immediate post-war decades a programme of architectural and garden restoration of Poland's most important palaces was put in place thanks to the campaigning and expertise of the garden historian and designer, Gerard Ciolek. He oversaw most of the work at various sites, including Wilanów, where the first phase of restoration, recreating a garden from surviving historical documents, was carried out in the years 1955-65, followed by a second phase during the 1960s.

The parterres have been replanted and given added symmetry by sentinel-like clipped yews. The old style of the original *parterres de broderie* has been put back in part, and elsewhere the beds are planted seasonally with spring tulips

BELOW
Streams wind their way between grassy banks and beneath trees and bridges in a scene that aspires to recreate nature at its most simple.

past is perpetuated in the sarcophagus over the pond and in the monument that commemorates the Battle of Raszyn in 1809, when the Poles fought tenaciously against the Austrians during the Napoleonic Wars.

Today the landscape at Wilanów evokes the romanticism that inspired its creation to a remarkable degree and impresses upon visitors the strength of the bond between such artistic expression and the Polish nation. It reminds them that shortly before the garden was completed, and prior to the three successive partitions of Poland by her neighbours Prussia, Austria, and Russia (who gained the most territory) in 1772, 1793, and 1795, the country was an independent monarchy. And yet it seems that the aggression of its neighbours inspired much of the artistic quality that appeared in Poland's romantic landscape gardens of the late 18th and early 19th centuries.

The painting of Wilanów (*see p. 97*) by Bernardo Bellotto records the palace and garden in their prime, when they were accorded similar status to the other great landscapes that he painted throughout Europe. That the garden has survived at all is quite remarkable, and it remains testimony to one of Europe's more troubled royal heritages and to the nation's ongoing pride in its past. After the end of its royal ownership Wilanów could have disappeared, but instead, two centuries later, it was proudly restored as a state property.

making way for summer annuals. But it is in the surrounding landscape garden that the place's history seems most undisturbed. Paths along avenues of lime trees or through woodland glades provide vistas across the lake and streams crossed by classical-style arched bridges and lead to vantage points decorated by some of the original baroque statues on their pedestals. Fortunately the most important architectural decorations survive, notably the open Chinese Temple that was taken from the design in Sir William Chambers' book *Design of Chinese Buildings*, published in 1757 and soon one of the most fashionable architectural and gardening books in Europe. Quite different, but equally intriguing, is the miniature mock castle, complete with arrow-slits and battlement; this stands beside the water and cleverly disguises a pump-house. The architectural variety is continued by a classical conservatory facing the lake and the different bridges across the various stretches of water.

The unity between the original formal gardens and the later landscape is one of the most distinctive features at Wilanów, demonstrated not only by the *patte d'oie* (junction) of avenues extending from one area to the other, but also by a long clipped hedge close to one side of the lake; this again draws the different features together. Outstanding trees throughout these gardens add greatly to the overall quality of plant life and ensure that at any time of year the atmosphere along the lake or the grassy stream banks is one of the utmost tranquillity. And, perhaps inevitably, the country's historical

ABOVE LEFT
The Chinese Temple, modelled on a design by Sir William Chambers, confirms the English origins to which the landscape designer looked for inspiration.

ABOVE
A springtime view when the lack of foliage on the trees gives an opportunity for the composition of the landscape to be enjoyed without distraction.

Wörlitz

DESSAU · GERMANY

Wörlitz, the creation of the anglophile Prince Franz von Anhalt-Dessau in the 18th century, proved to be a landscape garden of particular significance for a number of reasons. It was one of the first English-inspired landscape gardens in Europe and certainly the earliest to be made in Germany, marking a progression from the decorative baroque and rococo formal gardens to a style that other German garden-makers would follow with enthusiasm, although mostly not until the early 19th century. Because of its early inception, Wörlitz was to strongly influence a number of later royal and other parks in Germany, not least the park at Weimar created by Duke Karl August of Weimar with the help of his friend, the writer, dramatist, and poet Goethe.

Most significant for the future, the large-scale planning that Anhalt-Dessau carried out for an extensive landscape project, of which Wörlitz was just one element, provided the foundation for municipal park gardens that were developed in

RIGHT
The front of the Gothic House, the most theatrical of the various buildings that adorn the landscape, all which are modelled on English originals.

BELOW
A contemporary engraving looking across the lake called Kleines Walloch: an arcadian scene exactly as Prince Anhalt-Dessau would have intended.

Germany and then in the United States of America during the 19th century. In England many 18th-century landscapes, in particular in the work of the renowned English landscape gardener "Capability" Brown, incorporated productive agricultural and forestry land into a large-scale design that would cover hundreds of hectares. Anhalt-Dessau suggested that it was possible to similarly plan a whole area of countryside as a designed landscape and carried this to an extreme with the creation of the Gartenreich (Garden Kingdom), a series of interconnecting parks stretching for some 24km (15 miles) along the River Elbe.

By 1765 when he began the park at Wörlitz, the prince had long looked to liberal England for his inspiration. In 1764, on his first of a number of visits to England, one of his chief priorities was to see and study the great houses and gardens that were being created by the land-owning elite. As many of the buildings he later added to the landscape at Wörlitz confirm, he was never afraid to produce an almost exact replica – a sign of his increasing admiration for all things English. For nearly forty years he worked with the architect Friedrick Wilheim von Erdmansdorff, decorating and extending his landscape and integrating it with the others in

his principality. The house at Wörlitz designed by von Erdmansdorff was based on a model in *A Book of Architecture* by the classical architect James Gibbs, and just as the landscape garden set a precedent so too did this building because it was one of the first purely neoclassical houses in Germany.

The flat open plains that lie alongside the River Elbe were particularly susceptible to flooding, and when the new park at Wörlitz became submerged, much of the water was retained to form the first of two lakes, which provided focal points for the rest of the landscape design. The lakes were called the Kleines Walloch and the Grosses Walloch. Anhalt-Dessau revealed an unusually egalitarian attitude for his time by naming the landscape around the Kleines Walloch lake Schochgarten, after one of his gardeners, Johann Georg Schoch. The Neumark Garten was named after another of the prince's gardeners, Johann Christian Neumark. Both of these gardeners were involved in the development of the landscape, as was the Dessau court garden designer Johann Friedrich Eyserbeck.

The extraordinary range of garden buildings to be erected at Wörlitz in its first few years hinted at what was to come. These included the Nymphaeum, where an old ice-house was revived with an Ionic portico; the delightful Gothic House, which was modelled on the original at Shotover Park, near Oxford; the White Bridge built of wood over the Wolf Canal – a copy of Sir William Chambers' original Chinese Bridge in Kew Gardens; and the Temple of Venus, a domed open rotunda with similarities to Colin Campbell's Temple of Venus at Hall Barn, Buckinghamshire, and the Temple of Apollo at Stourhead, Wiltshire, designed by Henry Flitcroft.

The detail and accuracy of these reproductions meant that Anhalt-Dessau must have studied the originals in England in minute detail, so as to ensure their faithful construction back at Wörlitz. The quality of the work was so good that there was never any hint of pastiche, indeed it showed that the prince was taking the inspiration of the great English landscapes to a logical extreme. The imitations continued one of the many memorial and commemorative urns that he placed around the landscape in honour of friends and relatives was modelled on Alexander Pope's famous urn in his garden at Twickenham, Surrey. From the 1780s some of the sources of inspiration became more unusual. One temple is called the South Sea Pavilion because, as Patrick Bowe explained, "many of the

LEFT
Looking across one of the lakes towards the domed rotunda called the Temple of Venus (1794). This view is reminiscent of a view across the lake to the Temple of Apollo that can be seen in the great English landscape garden of Stourhead.

prince's English role-models had derived their wealth from the South Sea Company"; this despite the fact that many of them lost large portions of their wealth in the notorious venture. In 1790 the Synagogue was built, modelled on a circular church in Italy, and the following year Anhalt-Dessau commissioned a bridge, quite different to the one resembling the elegant original at Kew by Chambers, based on the Iron Bridge at Coalbrookdale in Staffordshire, celebrating the first recorded structure made of iron.

But the sheer size of the landscape ensured that the heterogeneous architecture could be happily accommodated, and any number of the views in the garden today, for instance along one of the tree-lined streams with a classical arched and balustraded bridge and the Synagogue in one direction, and the tower of the Gothic parish church in another, have a feel of total authenticity.

The prince's gardening tastes were not confined to the classical English landscape, and in one area he created his version of a "picturesque" garden that would have met with approval of late 18th-century enthusiasts in England. These parts were given strange, anthropological names such as the Skaldic Graves and included arrangements of enormous, rough boulders, artificial ruins, constructed rock faces, and caves. At the same time, he showed himself thoroughly in tune

with liberal, enlightened landscape-making with the creation of the Rousseau Island. Here, in the same style as the famous island at Ermenonville in France, he erected a memorial urn protected by a grove of poplar trees.

Even though most of Wörlitz's decorative buildings are not original, it does not detract from the overall fascination of the enormous landscape and the phenomenon that such an enthusiastic off-shoot of the English garden should emerge in 18th-century Germany. And it became, with the rest of the prince's work and his ideas set down in writing, one of the main influences on the development of landscape design in Germany through the 19th century. One of the most significant factors about the garden was how it had progressed from the priorities of the earlier 17th- and 18th-century gardens in Germany, to impress or entertain visitors, to the priority that would see its greatest expression in the picturesque movement, the deliberate evocation of different emotions.

Even while it was still being created, Wörlitz held visitors spellbound, not least one of the most distinguished, the playwright Goethe, who wrote in 1778: "Here it is now infinitely beautiful. It moved me very much yesterday evening as we crept through lakes, canals and woods, how the goods had allowed the prince to create a dream around himself. As one passes through it, it is as if one were being told a fairy tale, and has all the character of the Elysian Fields. In the gentlest multiplicity one thing flows into another, no height draw as one's eye and one's yearning towards a single point, one wanders about without asking whence one has gone or where one is coming."

ABOVE
Another architectural variation, this time an arched grotto that is shrouded by trees beside the water.

OPPOSITE
The white-painted, wooden, arched Chinese Bridge, modelled on Sir William Chambers' original in Kew Gardens, that spans one of the streams flowing between the lakes.

BOTANISTS & PLANTSMEN

THE EXPANSION OF KEW IN ENGLAND from the garden around a royal home to the premier botanical institution in the world is the ultimate illustration of what royal interest in horticulture can produce. But it is only one example; for centuries royal gardens all over Europe have been as notable for their high and innovative standards of horticulture as for their grandiose designs. Whether it was Frederick the Great tending his fruit at Sanssouci, Prince Albert designing the glasshouses for his favourite plants at Osborne House, or Leopold II choosing the rare palm trees and other exotic species for his glasshouses at Laeken, they all demonstrated a keenness that often produced spectacular results. As well as their personal enthusiasm for horticulture, various monarchs were in a unique position to use their patronage and, for centuries, unrivalled resources, to help benefit the development of gardens and horticulture whether through the introduction of new, often exotic, species of plants from overseas or a novel style of gardening that had originated in another country.

The extreme contrast to the botanical reputation of Kew is the privacy of Princess Sturdza's garden, Le Vasterival, close to the coast in northern France. Ever since the garden was begun in the late 1950s it has been increasingly well thought of by an initially small group of gardening cognoscenti, who knew about it and visited it regularly. Now open to the public it is firmly established as one of the most admired "plantsman's gardens" in Europe. This extraordinary garden demonstrates in exceptional style what has become a much-admired requirement in contemporary gardens, and this is an ability to show not only rare and unusual plants, but to combine suitable plants in a style that is not overtly formal or over designed. The harmony between plants and landscape is an elusive quality that Le Vasterival demonstrates to a rare degree.

Centuries earlier Princess Elizabeth, daughter of James I of Scotland, who in 1613 married Frederick the "Winter King" of Bohemia and the Elector of Palatine, was the patron of one

of the most significant early 17th century-gardens in Europe, the Hortus Palatinus. Through successive generations it has often been queens and princesses who have paid special attention to matters horticultural rather than ornamental. In some cases, such as the initiation of the first small botanical garden at Kew by Princess Augusta, or the patronage of the botanical artist Pierre-Joseph Redoute by the Empress Josephine, wife of Napoleon Bonaparte, the results have been of great significance in the development of botany and botanical art. In others it has ensured that flower gardens have been incorporated into a larger overall design, as for Maria Fedorovna at Pavlovsk and Maria Theresa at Schönbrunn, largely for their own personal enjoyment.

Throughout the book various gardens discussed would qualify for inclusion in this chapter, not least the gardens of Highgrove in England and Château de Belvédère in Belgium, both currently private homes of English and Belgian royalty and renowned for their flower gardens and other horticultural treasures. The late Queen Elizabeth the Queen Mother was reputed to love roses, and a number of new varieties were named after her. Less well known is her husband, George VI's passion for rhododendrons – a love that led to one of the most spectacular hybrid rhododendrons being named in his honour, *Rhododendron loderi* 'King George'.

It is in the horticultural and botanical fields that the transition in royal gardens, from private royal properties to state properties still often used by the royal family, but financed by the state in an appropriate manner and accessible to the public, has produced enormously beneficial results. Institutions such as Kew and Laeken are of international significance and will continue to make enormous contributions in the future. Other gardens, such as Osborne House, offer a tantalizing glimpse of the private taste of certain members of royal families and are fascinating as period pieces. Prince Albert was greatly interested by unusual trees, especially conifers, as they reminded him of his native Saxe-Coburg-Gotha in Germany. As a result, one of the delights at Osborne is his collection of trees that have now grown to maturity, including many that were newly introduced rarities at the time they were planted. In this way they demonstrated another advantage of royal privilege that occurred constantly; if a member of royalty showed an interest in acquiring a horticultural novelty or rarity, it was unlikely that the request would be refused.

LEFT
A summertime view along a grassy glade at Le Vasterival with planting combinations on both sides that exemplify the garden. The meandering path leading into the distance beckons.

RIGHT
During the 19th century Kew's new glasshouses provided a home for exotic, then rare, plants that astonished visitors at the same time as encouraging important botanical advances.

PREVIOUS PAGES
The rose garden at the Château de Belvédère, filled with Queen Paola's favourites, is one element in a very contemporary royal garden with its combination of privacy and plantsmanship.

Le Park du Vasterival

DIEPPE · FRANCE

In the contemporary period royal gardeners have often made their own gardens rather than employing designers and architects. They have followed the contemporary desire to make gardens that combine the personality of their creator with plantsmanship, producing places of privacy rather than places of display.

There can be few gardens anywhere in Europe that reflect the personality and taste of their creator so strongly as Le Vasterival, made by Princess Sturdza during the second half of the 20th century. Norwegian by birth, the princess has created one of the most remarkable contemporary gardens to be found anywhere, dependent purely on the quality and variety of its plants and their arrangement and association.

When she purchased the property 1km (¾ mile) from the sea just west of the French port of Dieppe in 1957, the site of the garden was untamed countryside, covered in undergrowth and open to the winds that blew in relentlessly from the sea. And yet the seaside position gave the garden a wonderfully mild microclimate that the princess appreciated from the outset, and which she knew could be complemented by controlling the winds with shelter belts of trees and shrubs. These were the first things to be planted but, as with all future planting, the natural, undulating shape of the landscape was clearly retained without alteration. Royal gardens of the past have often involved transforming the natural landscape; here the opposite was the chief priority.

The garden is immediately remarkable for its total lack of formality or ornament: there are no symmetrical borders, no clipped hedges, and no sculptures, buildings, or other ornamental decoration. Instead, the princess has built up colonies and associations of plants within an overall natural, woodland style. Within the protective shelter belt a mixture of trees including ash, birch, oak, and pine provide the garden's framework. Paths and glades that vary in shape and size follow the undulating contours of the ground so that planting and landscape merge in a manner to which many contemporary gardens aspire.

Princess Sturdza has been quoted as advocating, "work for the plant; work ten times over to plant", and for many visitors to her garden the qualities of plantsmanship are its most fascinating aspect. Everywhere you look, the plants exude healthiness, and as one commentator has written: "That the plants at Le Vasterival grow luxuriantly, that their flowering season is longer than elsewhere, is due neither to the humid Normandy climate, nor to any special quality in the soil, and certainly not to specific treatments or fertilizers for the plants.

OPPOSITE
Different foliage shapes mass together on either side of a narrow pathway, providing a dense layer of planting beneath trees and shrubs. Look between the plants to glimpse at other areas of the garden.

The Princess's unequivocal success is due to the close attention that she pays to the planting, pruning, and aftercare of every plant, shrub, and tree."

Today the garden is remarkable for the enormous collection of plants, and yet they are planted together so naturally and easily that there is no sense of them having been gathered to form a collection. One of Princess Sturdza's great skills has been her plant associations, combining groups containing a range of sizes, from trees to creeping groundcover. Trees and shrubs abound in seemingly limitless variety with highlights such as cherries, cornus, rhododendrons, maples, and viburnums. In addition there are smaller euphorbias, hellebores, and hostas. The mixture of plants in the different areas of the garden is matched by the seasonal combinations so that at every time of the year there is visual interest and beauty. The combined effect exemplifies the creation of plant colonies that has been the goal of many contemporary gardens; combinations of shape, foliage, and colour that are carefully planned but mature to look disarmingly natural.

The garden has evolved with a balanced eye for both the welfare of individual plants and the combined effect, and it is for this reason that at any given time of the year there seem to be no gaps from one week to the next. Princess Sturdza would admit to few favourites in the plant world, instead when planning for any season, be it late winter or early autumn, she thinks of combinations in all stages, from groundcover to bulbs, perennials, climbers, shrubs, and trees. Many of the oldest trees in the garden have grown up to provide the woodland conditions under which many of the plants thrive; later additions have included the array of flowering trees, which as much as any others in the garden confirm the princess's discerning eye. Rarely, if ever, are these trees,

whether an unusual Japanese prunus, a magnolia, or a sorbus, chosen and positioned to say "look at me". Instead, they form part of a group – albeit often the most immediately striking – and as a result confirm the sense of integration as the visitor looks from one area of the garden to another.

For Princess Sturdza the individual quality and health of the plants has always been the abiding priority. No matter how many thousands of plants the garden may contain, they are all nurtured to the maximum degree. Careful preparation of the ground before planting, the actual planting process, constant application of compost, the removal of competition from weeds, and pruning only to cut out unhealthy or unwanted growth all contribute to the overall effect. Whether large or small, plants are encouraged as part of a community, and this greatly enhances the sense of unity both in separate groups and from one area to another.

The result, and perhaps the most skilful achievement, is a garden that conceals all the efforts, planning, and maintenance to make it appear as though it has evolved naturally, without human intervention. On closer inspection it is clear that such variety of planting for damp and dry conditions, light and shade, for winter colour, or to create a vista could never have come about of its own accord. But during a period when many gardeners have been most interested in the relationship between the man-made garden and the qualities of nature, of plants thriving in the wild, Le Vasterival has shown a shining light as to how enormous horticultural knowledge can be applied to such effect. Without doubt the skill that has been applied by the princess and the intensely personal nature of the garden will be its greatest challenge in the future, and is what sets it apart from other, grander royal gardens that were deliberately created for posterity.

LEFT
Rhododendrons beside water whose other edges are lined with aquatic plants, making a tranquil scene where the planting seems to enhance nature in a way characteristic of the garden as a whole.

RIGHT
Early spring at Le Vasterival sees a succession of flowering trees, the colours of their delicate blossoms accentuated by the fact that there are still no leaves on the other trees.

Royal Botanic Gardens, Kew

LONDON · ENGLAND

K ew is a royal garden of arguably unique interest and distinction as a result of having made the transition from being a favoured royal home during the 18th century to becoming the premier botanical institution in the world during the 19th century, a position that it has continued to hold ever since. It is not the oldest botanical garden in England – that distinction goes to Oxford University where the Botanic Garden was established in 1621; just over 50 years later, in 1673, the Chelsea Physic Garden was founded in London. But for historical interest and the combination of different garden styles with overriding botanical and horticultural importance, it has no rival.

The story begins during the reign of James I, who had a hunting-lodge in the Old Deer Park of Richmond, close to the present Kew Gardens. Nearly a century later, William III employed George London, one half of the most-renowned gardening partnership at the turn of the 18th century with Henry Wise, to create a small formal garden beside the house. During Queen Anne's reign the house was let, but in 1718 the then Prince of Wales, who went on to become George II, decided to use the house as a regular home. It was renamed Richmond Lodge, and during the 1730s, by which time the prince had ascended to the throne, was rebuilt by William Kent. It was the king's wife, Queen Caroline, who ensured that the garden would be a major priority, for she brought a direct

OPPOSITE
An impressive seasonal display of tulips and wallflowers in front of the great Palm House at Kew, for over a century the first home to a host of exotic species newly introduced to England.

BELOW
Joshua Kirby's view of the White House (Kew House) as rebuilt by William Kent for Prince Frederick, whose wife, Princess Augusta, initiated the adjacent botanic garden.

connection with another major royal garden, Charlottenburg near Berlin (*see pp.*158–61), where she had been brought up as Princess Caroline Brandenberg-Anspach. She employed Charles Bridgeman, who in 1728 had succeeded Henry Wise as the royal gardener, to create a new garden, and through her enthusiasm the size of the Kew estate grew to some 160ha (400 acres), much larger than it is today.

An intriguing feature of today's Kew is that it is made up of what were originally two adjacent royal gardens. The second was begun around the home that King George and Queen Caroline's son and daughter-in-law, Frederick, Prince of Wales and Princess Augusta of Saxe-Gotha, made around the house they took on called the White House, which was demolished in 1802 but stood close to the present Dutch house or Kew Palace. Throughout his adult life, until his early death in 1751 aged 44, the Prince of Wales was in open conflict with his parents, who in 1737 actually banned him from court. The household that he and Princess Augusta established was in constant rivalry with that of his parents, and

the close proximity of their homes at Richmond and Kew, and their mutual interest in gardening, especially for the queen and Princess Augusta, ensured that there would be a competitive edge in their development.

After the death of her husband Princess Augusta established herself as the most significant royal person in the development of Kew for two reasons. First she commissioned the architect Sir William Chambers to design and build a series of 25 garden buildings, of which five survive today as some of the most memorable features at Kew. Second, with the advice of her husband's friend, Lord Bute, who would become tutor to their son, George III, under whom he would serve as prime minister, she began the botanical collection that would continue to grow thereafter. The five remaining buildings by Chambers are the Orangery, the Temple of Arethusa, the Temple of Bellona, the Ruined Arch and, most famous of all, the Pagoda, which rises to 50m (164ft) and is a landmark from miles around. After the accession of her son in 1760, "Capability" Brown, who in 1764 became royal gardener at

LEFT
The saucer-like leaves of one of the plant-wonders of the Victorian age from South America, Victoria amazonica *(named after the Queen and originally called* Victoria regia*).*

RIGHT
Inside Decimus Burton's Palm House the exotic foliage of palms and other plants is complemented by the decorative ironwork of railings and balustrades.

ABOVE
In contrast to the grandeur and its many dramatic plants Kew has plenty of intimate spots where more modest plant combinations can be enjoyed.

OPPOSITE
Whether growing tender exotics in the 19th century or organically tended wild-flower meadows, as shown here, Kew has always been in the vanguard of gardening development.

Hampton Court, was commissioned to landscape the gardens around Richmond Lodge, where Queen Caroline's original garden was swept away – no doubt a source of satisfaction to the ageing Princess Augusta, who died in 1772.

King George III took over his mother's home, and a year later saw the introduction of the man who would guarantee Kew's future, Sir Joseph Banks. A keen botanist from a young age, Banks was a man of wealth and strong connections. In 1768 he accompanied Captain Cook on his epic voyage aboard the *Endeavour*, taking with him a botanical team who recorded their discoveries. George III entrusted him with the management of Kew, and within a few years, Princess Augusta's collection had not only been organized, but greatly expanded. In the year of his arrival alone some 800 different species were planted. Equally significant, he initiated the plant-collecting trips to far corners of the world that would, in the 19th century, provide Kew with the rarities and new arrivals that secured its pre-eminent position. The first expedition was to the Cape Province in South Africa, where Banks dispatched Francis Masson during the 1770s. Masson's most exotic introduction to the garden from this trip was named *Strelitzia regina*, after George III's wife, Charlotte of Mecklenburg-Strelitz.

In 1802 Banks organized for the gardens of Kew and Richmond to be united, and six years after his death in 1820 Prince Puckler-Muskau, a knowledegable gardener and keen traveller wrote that Kew, "unquestionably possesses the most complete collection of exotic plants in Europe". Following the death of both Banks and George III in the same year Kew's fortunes declined, but in 1837, the year of Queen Victoria's accession, a survey of the royal gardens carried out for the Treasury recommended that Kew was made into a "scientific and horticultural institution worthy of the nation".

Four years later, in 1841, the distinguished botanist Sir William Hooker was appointed the first director and he was succeeded by his son, Sir Joseph in 1865. The four decades of their tenure witnessed both regular plant-collecting expeditions all over the world and the further development of the gardens, not least to enhance their scientific status. In 1876 the Jodrell Laboratory was built, and in 1882 the Marianne North Gallery, which was designed by James Fergusson, was added. Three years earlier North had offered Hooker her paintings and the gallery. In 1844 Decimus Burton was commissioned to begin the Palm House, which remains one of Kew's great landmarks, followed by his Temperate House, completed in 1898. The gardens were largely redesigned by William Nesfield, whose masterly work linked the new glasshouses to the older gardens with a series of three main vistas. He was responsible for the parterres around the glasshouses.

During the 20th century Kew's most notable addition was the Princess of Wales House, named after Diana, Princess of Wales, and opened in 1987. In 1965 the gardens expanded to a second location with the tenancy of Wakehurst Place in Surrey. Today the combination of history, gardening architecture, and planting on a regal scale, with scientific research that remains in the vanguard of modern botany and horticulture, ensure that Kew's remarkable reputation continues unchallenged.

BELOW
William Marlow's contemporary view of Sir William Chambers' Pagoda with two other of his buildings that have disappeared, left the Alhambra and right the Mosque.

RIGHT
More than two centuries after it was built the Pagoda remains Kew's dominant landmark, accentuated by the alignment of the main vistas in Nesfield's 19th-century alterations.

Osborne House

ISLE OF WIGHT · ENGLAND

Osborne is a shrine to Queen Victoria and her husband, Prince Albert. It was without doubt their favourite home in England (only Balmoral in Scotland rivalled it) and the place where, in January 1901, the 81-year-old queen died. They bought Osborne in 1845 specifically to have a country house where they could enjoy privacy, and because of its situation overlooking the Solent - the channel between the the Isle of Wight and the mainland. Developments continued until Prince Albert's death in 1861, most of which were his ideas.

In all matters domestic, Queen Victoria was happy if Albert was happy, and her early enthusiasm for Osborne in a letter of April 1845 to her prime minister, Lord Melbourne, confirms this: "It is impossible to imagine a prettier spot – valley and woods which would be beautiful anywhere; but all this near the sea (the woods grow into the sea) is quite perfection; we have a charming beach quite to ourselves. The sea was so blue and calm that the Prince said it was like Naples. And then we can walk out anywhere without fear of being followed and mobbed."

In partnership with the architect, Thomas Cubitt, Prince Albert was responsible for the design of the new house in Italianate style with its distinctive clock tower at one end. The design of the terraced gardens was almost exclusively the

OPPOSITE
One of the highly ornamental terraces planned in Italianate style by Prince Albert to provide a suitable setting for the house that he conceived as a seaside villa.

BELOW
The royal family in the gardens of Osborne in the last years of Queen Victoria's reign. Standing behind the Queen is her grandson, later George V, with his eldest son, who became Edward VIII.

Prince's, laid out to the north of the house with views out over the Solent beyond. Although devoted to Queen Victoria, Prince Albert always remained loyal to his native Germany. For the garden at Osborne he consulted an expert whose opinions he valued on all matters artistic, Professor Ludwig Gruner of Dresden, and the final results incorporated some intriguing Germanic touches with highly ornamented Italianate formality. Around tall fountain basins surmounted by figures of Venus and other Classical deities, flowerbeds, some with the additional feature of a clipped topiary stag, were laid out. The pattern of gravel paths, lawn, and bedding was restored during the 1990s.

As Prince Albert had a strong sense of what was appropriate for any situation, the garden around the house was given over to formal terraces. But he was also a keen botanist, and his fascination with different species of trees resulted in the outstanding specimens planted in parts of the garden and out into the park beyond – a mixture of deciduous and exotic conifers, as was the fashion in the 19th century. He was also devoted to the broad education of his children to which end he organized for a Swiss Cottage to be imported to Osborne from Switzerland and set up in the garden. Some distance from the house this became the focus of his horticultural education of the children. They were taught to grow vegetables in their own little plots, and he encouraged them by offering to purchase their ripe produce.

Prince Albert loved Osborne because it was warm and beside the sea – as Disraeli, one of Victoria's favourite prime ministers, wrote after a visit: "A Sicilian palazzo with gardens, terraces, statues, and vases shining in the sun, than which nothing can be conceived more captivating." He also loved it because it was his and Victoria's; he didn't feel he was treading on the toes of royal protocol and centuries of establishment as was sometimes the case at Windsor Castle. With Cubitt's help he designed the glasshouses in the walled kitchen garden, and this, along with the whole garden, has been restored by English Heritage, the work designed and carried out by Rupert Golby. Within a symmetrical design and maintaining the kitchen garden tradition of productivity and display (the walls support trained fruit trees, and vegetables mix with the flowers), Golby's idea was to give a vibrantly modern picture, but using plants known to have been popular during the Victorian era and maximizing the garden's warm seaside climate by growing exotics, such as luxuriant clumps of arum lilies.

In high summer the result of Golby's work is a kaleidoscope that Victoria and Albert would have certainly enjoyed; as in his day, Albert's glasshouses are again filled with exotic annual plants, now all originating from South Africa. The use of the entwined V and A motif on terracotta pots, garden seats, and decorative ironwork is a constant reminder to visitors of the garden's original creators and their enjoyment of it.

OPPOSITE
Prince Albert's prize and joy, the Swiss Cottage, imported from Switzerland for his children and now adorned with new flower gardens.

ABOVE
The high summer zenith of Golby's vibrant planting in the restored walled garden at Osborne, with Prince Albert's glasshouse in the background.

Château de Belvédère

BRUSSELS · BELGIUM

Château de Belvédère is a haven of peaceful privacy that many people would find hard to believe, situated as it is in the suburbs of Brussels only a short distance from the main city area. The garden exudes tranquillity and is full of qualities that reflect the active interest of Belgium's Queen Paola, whose husband became King Albert II in 1993. She has transformed what she found when she first went to live at Belvédère, during the 1970s, and to achieve her aims she enlisted the help of her friend, the leading international garden designer, Arabella Lennox-Boyd, who is, like the queen, an Italian by birth.

Much of Belvédère's atmosphere derives from the fact that it has always been a private home, never an official residence or open to the public. The house, whose elegant neoclassical style reflects its name, was built towards the end of the 18th century by Edouard, Viscount de Walckiers. He was a businessman who was clearly a devoted supporter of the royal family, for shortly

RIGHT
The central yew-hedged octagon in the middle of Lennox-Boyd's new garden combines formality and intimacy. Inviting gateways lead to other areas of the garden.

BELOW
The château's distinctive dome and pillared façade provide an elegant backdrop for views from the garden. Wisteria floribunda 'Alba' flourishes over the pergola in the foreground.

before his death in 1837 he presented them with the Château de Belvédère as a gift. A formal garden made during the 19th century has been transformed into Queen Paola's new garden created during the last thirty years.

The château enjoys an elevated position with a small park falling away in one direction with views to the city of Brussels beyond. The large rectangular terrace, to which stone steps lead from the house, was filled with a pattern of small box-edged flowerbeds planted with Hybrid Tea roses. From her first visit Lennox-Boyd felt that the existing design spoilt the relationship between the château and the view and that it needed to be changed; happily Queen Paola shared her view. "Looking down from the windows of the château, I was struck by how grim this parterre looked, particularly when seen in relation to the landscape beyond; and when walking on the terrace I felt no sense of space or belonging. This rigid, sparse design did not suit the Queen, who had a keen interest in plants and colour combinations and a penchant for English gardens such as Sissinghurst and Hidcote which she visited

regularly. She wanted a more intimate garden in which she could indulge her love of plants: a garden with a profusion of flowers and scent."

The surrounding areas of the garden and the park with which it merges are blessed with many fine trees, which have been added to by successive generations of the royal family. In some parts they frame the long views across the garden and park; closer to the château they have provided the framework for the new design that Lennox-Boyd has carried out for the queen to replace the rose parterre. Part of the quality derives from the fact that this, the most important area in the whole garden, was conceived and set out as a whole, and the unity of the component parts is instantly recognizable. The garden was also carefully planned to be personal, incorporating features that Queen Paola particularly liked and including her favourite plants.

One problem with the rose parterre was how uninteresting it had looked for many months of the year when the roses were not in flower, especially in winter and early

spring. A priority for the new design was to incorporate features for year-round interest, and this was done primarily with the use of box and yew evergreen, which also provide the framework. The overall pattern that the queen hoped to achieve was a horticultural variation of a Persian carpet, with a brilliant mixture of colours interwoven into the yew and box, as Lennox-Boyd has described. "The pattern of the 'carpet' would be made up of yew and box hedges combined with trees, and many different flowering plants would give it colour. Tall, thick yew hedges would define the planted areas. Each was to have a different character. Some would have brick paths laid in different geometric patterns."

To break up the old uniformity and yet retain the degree of formality that the garden required Lennox-Boyd planned contrasting treatments for the two long sides flanking the terrace garden as you descend from the steps. On one side a long metal pergola is swathed in early summer with the luxuriant tresses of white-flowered *Wisteria floribunda* 'Alba'; along the other is a parallel walk between pleached limes, which are underplanted with small spring bulbs. While the lime walk is in a style reminiscent of the famous one at Sissinghurst, it is also entirely suitable because, "lime *allées* are traditional to Belgium".

In the main formal area only the circular pool at the far end from the château was retained from the old design and incorporated into the new one, for which the aim was to create a series of interlinked, but quite individual, garden rooms in a plan that overcomes the previous flat regularity. In the words of the designer: "Seen from above, the area has a formal, geometric grandeur with a pattern and central

LEFT
The elegant symmetry of the pleached lime walk is complemented by the sparkling array of spring flowers that are planted in the borders below.

ABOVE
Box spirals were moved to the middle of the new garden to give a sense of maturity. Their pale green contrasts with the darker central yew.

motif, but as you walk into the design, the impression changes and you find yourself in a garden with several enclosures, each intimate and private. Once you are inside, the spaces enfold you and you are no longer aware of the house or anything else outside."

The central motif Lennox-Boyd mentions is an area of lawn enclosed by yew hedges forming an octagon with a topiary pattern in the middle. Box domes clipped into spirals were moved to here from elsewhere in the garden and they stand in a circle around a taller central yew clipped similarly into a tiered pattern. The formality of the clipped evergreens is softened by plantings of roses and wild flowers. The octagonal yew hedges have openings onto the central vista from the château and at right angles to this, but the most ingenious feature is the set of four gateways positioned into each length of hedge, all enclosed by yew clipped into a classical pediment. Passing through any of these gateways gives the impression of entering a room, and they lead out into the four individual

ABOVE
The old pool has been rejuvenated by its new position as the unexpected focus at one end of the garden and by the abundances of irises around its edge.

gardens, all the same size and shape but each different: an old-fashioned rose garden, a yellow garden, an early-summer garden, and a fruit-and-herb garden.

The early-summer garden has four beds, each planted with a beautifully shaped crab-apple tree, *Malus tschonoskii*, and divided by brick-patterned paths. On entering the small area it is obvious that the plants have been carefully chosen, many for a combination of flower and scent such as the two *Viburnum carlesii* that stand on either side of the entrance, or for scale, such as the shrubby *Prunus glandulosa* 'Alba Plena'. There is also subtle variation in scale, from the small flowering trees and shrubs already mentioned to a variety of perennials and other flowering plants for different seasons. Most are chosen because they are favourites of the queen's: early-spring hellebores giving way to pulmonarias, euphorbias, and wallflowers. Different irises include *Iris* 'Amethyst Flame' and *I.* 'Black Taffeta', which are followed by peonies such as *Paeonia lactiflora* 'White Wings', the tree peony *P.* x *lemoinei* 'Souvenir

de Maxime Cornu', and the soft-shaded flowers of *Deutzia* 'Avalanche'. The yellow garden mixes single-colour flowers of many different hues with golden and yellow foliage and, as Lennox-Boyd suggests: "The concentration of one-colour planting is very effective in a small space and yellow can be particularly successful." There are beds dominated by yellow-flowered roses, such as *Rosa* 'Norwich Union', and others with flowering plants, including *Cytisus battandieri* and yellow lupins mixing with the rich yellow-green foliage of the small tree *Robinia pseudoacacia* 'Frisia' and the sword-like leaves of variegated yuccas.

In midsummer the rose garden has a wonderfully nostalgic atmosphere, again because within a small space a quantity of old-fashioned shrub roses are concentrated. They spill out of the beds that surround a central lawn, and many of Queen Paola's favourites are grown here, such as the repeat-flowering *Rosa* 'Reine des Violettes' and *R.* 'Comte de Chambord'. Other particular favourites include some of the best old-fashioned varieties: 'Fantin-Latour', 'Maiden's Blush', 'Louise Odier', 'Ispahan', 'Tuscany Superba', 'Hippolyte', and 'The Bishop'. They are underplanted with creamy Regal lilies, as well as a carefully chosen selection of foliage perennials including hostas, helichrysum, salvias, and stachys. The last garden has developed into a miniature potager in an immaculate pattern, outlined by espalier apples and pears and beds filled with small-scale plants such as alpine strawberries and herbs, including different hyssops and thymes, or flowers such as lily-of-the-valley.

The central path through the garden enclosures emerges between yew hedges at the far end from the château to the old circular pool, which has been brought into the overall scheme and transformed by new planting. In two semicircles around are flowering cherry trees between which yew hedges have been planted in lines towards the pool. Under the cherries and extending in some places into the water's edge are clumps of yellow and purple Siberian irises, planted in single colours to enhance their effect. On the far side a wooden seat beckons, and from here the view extends back through the series of yew hedges and enclosures to the dome of the château beyond.

Given its position in front of the château the parterre has always been the most important feature of the garden at Belvédère, and its redesign has transformed its overall appearance. But in the manner of many of the best contemporary gardens, the combination of well-ordered design and exuberant planting is also a contrast to larger-scale informally planned areas that surround it. The change from walking along one of the intimate yew-hedged paths in the parterre gardens and emerging to the spacious walks across open, sloping lawn planted with specimen trees and spring bulbs is enjoyable at any time of year.

Everything about the garden at the Château de Belvédère confirms that it has always been, primarily, a private garden for personal enjoyment. It has been created to complement the delightful small-scale architecture of the house, which is an immediate contrast to the great palaces that are found in so many royal gardens, and to take advantage of the natural qualities of the landscape in the park. The improvements to

LEFT
A wooden pergola, soon to be draped with climbing roses, crosses one of the garden's immaculate gravel paths, whose edges are softened by clumps of lavender thriving in the sunny conditions.

TOP
In spring and, here, in autumn, the wider areas of lawns and the trees leading into parkland take on particular qualities and provide memorable views to the château.

ABOVE
In the woodland the evening sunlight dapples the grass and flowers around two unsuspecting ornamental birds, creating a scene of undisturbed tranquillity that typifies the garden.

the formal but unexciting design means that the garden now has something to offer at all times of the year.

As with Prince Charles at Highgrove in England (*see pp.196–201*), Queen Paola is a passionate gardener with favourite plants and styles of design. As Prince Charles has done with different designers and craftsmen, so the Belgian queen in partnership with Lennox-Boyd has sought to create a garden that is both new and exciting and yet in harmony with its older house and setting. This has also meant that since the new garden was begun in the 1970s it has steadily evolved because of the queen's constant attention. As borders and plant groups have matured, subtle changes have been made with new plants being introduced and others moved or taken out because they do not suit a certain scheme or grow too large. The luxury of privacy enables the garden to be developed like this, in the way of gardening enthusiasts all over Europe, and means that for those fortunate enough to be able to visit the immediate message is that this has been made, first and foremost, by a garden-lover rather than by a member of a royal family. It is instantly recognizable as the garden surrounding a home rather than a garden created for an offical residence, and this gives a certain informality to the mood and atmosphere.

GREAT
RESTORATIONS

MANY GARDENS IN THIS BOOK survive today in a restored or reconstructed form. With gardens that are centuries old this is inevitable, and since the mid-20th century there has been a growing concern to preserve many different aspects of European culture among which gardens feature highly. The gardens of Peterhof, Pavlovsk, and Tsarskoye Selo in Russia were all meticulously reconstructed along with their palaces to emphasize the iniquity of their destruction during World War II, as was the case with Charlottenburg in Germany.

In other gardens periods of neglect have led to partial restoration whether of certain features, such as statuary, or the inevitable replanting of trees to replace original specimens that have reached the end of their natural life. Many of the formal gardens described in this book depend on lofty avenues to mark out their vistas and axes; frequently, whether at Fredensborg in Denmark, Aranjuez in Spain, or Versailles in France, the lines are marked out for the future with trees planted as replacements during the last hundred years or so.

There are some gardens, however, where recent restoration projects have had particular significance, which has enhanced their character and reputation, and nowhere more than at Het Loo in the Netherlands and Hampton Court in England. The fact that they were both largely created by the same monarchs, William III and his wife Queen Mary, heightens the interest of their restoration. In these cases exhaustive research was carried out into the originals, both in archives and archaeological work on site, and as a result the restoration achieved an extraordinary degree of accuracy. They both confirm that with gardens of sufficient importance the need for restoration to preserve their original features of design, ornament, and planting far outweighs any criticism that might in the past have been levelled against them as unoriginal pastiches far better swept away and replaced with something new. In today's gardens there should be room for the new and the old, with the distance of time growing with every generation, a genuine example of a great garden from a distant period will only grow in importance and fascination.

Different styles of restoration are illustrated in the gardens of Isola Bella in Italy and Beloeil in Belgium. For centuries the former has been one of the most charismatic of all Italian gardens, thanks to its position and dramatic design. The restoration carried out in recent decades has included new planting that enhances the original. As a result the garden has a newly found vitality, ensuring that far from declining into being an ornamental relic it has taken on a new life as a garden combining the best of its Renaissance original with a complementary contemporary layer.

Today's gardens are by necessity usually limited in size compared to the great gardens of the past. So a landscape such as Beloeil, where the scale is pre-eminent and the individual ornamental features are designed to play a subdued part in an overall scheme, is unusual and challenging. The garden's abiding quality is the simple interplay of formally arranged trees, water, and grass with the focal feature of the château, and the degree to which the garden's restoration has been carried out to enhance this in the spirit of the original is remarkable.

The restoration of a royal garden demonstrates the extent to which continuity of ownership is often their best defence. Centuries of establishment and a degree of acknowledged importance by virtue of this puts them in a position that few other gardens enjoy. Today, especially, gardens are most often under threat when their ownership changes. Royal gardens are in a privileged position by comparison, and in many cases the immaculate condition of their restored status is the most emphatic confirmation of this.

OPPOSITE
The major restoration at Hampton Court has been in the Privy Garden, but other areas have also been restored including the Tudor Knot Garden.

LEFT
A view from the parterre to the terraces at Isola Bella shows the combination of plants and statuary that make the garden so vibrant today.

PREVIOUS PAGES
A patterned detail from the parterre at Het Loo, where the formal gardens have undergone one of the most extensive restorations of recent decades.

Hampton Court

LONDON · ENGLAND

Although no longer used as an official residence by the British royal family, Hampton Court is owned by the Historic Royal Palaces Trust and remains, indisputably, England's supreme royal garden, where five centuries of continuous history and development have been crowned in recent years by outstanding restoration. It is as part of the palace and gardens' long, unbroken history that the restoration work achieves its true significance.

Hampton Court's current history began in 1514, when the then all-powerful Cardinal Wolsey leased the manor including the two adjacent parks, Home and Bushy Park, which extended to some 800ha (1975 acres). Wolsey soon created one of the most lavish of all Tudor houses, with gardens below his private apartments on the south side facing the River Thames. But in a fateful point of comparison, it appeared that his desire for splendour backfired in the same way that it would for Nicolas Fouquet, a similarly powerful French minister, during the reign of Louis XIV. After Henry VIII had visited Wolsey at Hampton Court in 1525 he was clearly jealous of his cardinal's magnificent house; within the year he had taken control of the palace and grounds, and Wolsey's downfall had begun. Just over a century later Fouquet's palace and gardens at Vaux-le-Vicomte incurred Louis XIV's wrath, and the French minister's ruin followed swiftly.

LEFT
A panoramic view of the restored Privy Garden stretching away from Wren's south façade, looking much as it did when it was first created some 300 years ago.

RIGHT
Queen Mary's Bower, the long covered walk along one terrace overlooking the Privy Garden. It had disappeared but has been rebuilt to replicate the original.

Henry VIII extended the Tudor palace and gardens on the south side, as well as stocking the parks for hunting and adding a tiltyard for the jousting contests, which as a young man he loved to watch. Hampton Court was the scene of his turbulent courtships with successive wives, Anne Boleyn, Jane Seymour, and Catherine Howard. Jane Seymour died at the palace, and Catherine Howard was arrested here before her execution on Tower Hill in 1542.

Some changes were made to the gardens during Charles I's reign, but it was not until the end of the Civil War and the restoration of his son, Charles II, in 1660, that new developments were carried out to a great extent. Charles had spent much of the war in exile in France, where, like many other Englishmen, he had admired the great formal gardens being created by Louis XIV and his grandest nobles. At Hampton Court he determined to have a garden to rival Louis XIV's Versailles, and the work was directed by his gardener, John Rose, who had studied under André Le Nôtre, the designer responsible for the layout of Versailles. Rose was assisted by the French gardeners Gabriel and André Mollet, who also worked for the king at St James's Palace, and who designed the superb *patte d'oie* of lime avenues that still extend from the east of Hampton Court. The three avenues radiate out from a semicircular garden in front of the palace; the long canal was dug along the central avenue.

It was during the reign of William III and Queen Mary that Hampton Court reached its zenith. They employed Sir Christopher Wren to extend the palace with a new building around the enclosed fountain court, of which two sides now form the south and east façades of the main palace. William's private apartments were in the former, Mary's in the latter, and the gardens they looked out over were to be as important as the new building. To the east Charles II's *patte d'oie* design was completed by the addition of the Great Fountain Garden, a pattern of parterres and fountain pools filling the large semicircular garden, which was designed by Daniel Marot. To the south, between the palace and the river, the old gardens were swept away and replaced by the baroque Privy Garden, which led to a magnificent curving wrought-iron screen on the riverside by Jean Tijou. The Privy Garden was divided by gravel paths into four symmetrical sections focusing on a central pool, each with its own marble statue and pattern of grass, gravel, and clipped yew.

William III had more ambitious plans for Hampton Court, but they were interrupted by the death of Mary in 1694 and came to an end with his death in 1702, which marked the beginning of a long period of relative decline. Queen Anne did not like Hampton Court and took out most of the fountains and parterres from Marot's semicircular garden on the south side; her Hanoverian successors used the palace during the reign

of George I, but after the death of George II's wife Caroline in 1737, it was effectively abandoned. Final acknowledgment that it would no longer be used as a royal residence came in 1838, when Queen Victoria announced that the state apartments and gardens would be open to the public.

Restoration work designed to recreate specific areas of the garden in their original style began during the 1920s, when the Elizabethan knot garden was laid out on the south side of the palace, in a small rectangle in front of where the old Tudor building joins Wren's later addition; this faithfully recreated a similar garden that had existed during Elizabeth I's reign. Later, the sunken Pond Garden, originally made by Cardinal Wolsey and enjoyed by William and Mary, who built the battlemented Banqueting House on its far side looking over the river, was restored as a formal flower garden bedded out in patterns with annuals.

The decision during the 1990s, however, to restore the Privy Garden, suggested that much of Hampton Court's original period appearance would be revived. The work was begun in 1995 after painstaking archaeological research, and

ABOVE
The enclosed sunken Pond Garden was part of the Tudor original; today it is overlooked by William III's Banqueting House and has been restored to its original state.

OPPOSITE
Kynff's bird's-eye view of Hampton Court in its full glory at the turn of the 18th century before the later simplifications to the formal designs.

recreated one of the outstanding French baroque-inspired gardens in England. The original garden had begun to disappear with alterations during the 19th century, and, as the changes made at this time grew to increasing maturity, the 17th-century design effectively vanished. Instead of a formal, open pattern, views from the palace were virtually obscured by shrubberies that had grown up in the flowerbeds and Tijou's screen was all but invisible from the garden.

Extraordinarily, given that some three centuries had elapsed, excavations revealed much of the old Privy Garden's original pattern of footings, and this, along with the contemporary views and accounts of the garden, allowed for a recreation of unusual accuracy. The dimensions of the areas were restored, and the original patterns, focusing on the quartet of marble statues and the central fountain pool, were recreated. On both sides the raised terrace walks were rebuilt, and the one dividing the Privy and Pond gardens was given the covered trellised walk that had been build for William III's wife, Mary II, and named Queen Mary's Bower. At the far end the final flourish was to return the gilding to the central panels of Tijou's wrought-iron screen.

The transformation wrought by the restoration was drastic, but after a few years it has clearly succeeded in recreating the appearance and atmosphere of the period when the palace was extended by Wren for William and Mary. And while the Privy Garden had, effectively disappeared, to the east of the palace the bones of the original layout, the great lime avenues, the canal, and the semicircular area immediately in front remain. If other areas of the garden received similar treatment to the Privy Garden, such as replacing the overgrown yews with small clipped ones or recreating Marot's dazzling fountain display and parterres, the restoration of Hampton Court's former glory would be complete. Nonetheless, it is remarkable that three centuries after the artist Leonard Knyff painted his panoramic bird's-eye view of Hampton Court in 1702 (*see p.140*), much of the detail that he portrayed is today instantly recognizable.

Hampton Court retains some of the oldest features of any royal garden in Europe and more than any other garden in Britain it represents that country's contribution to the golden age of monarchical gardens. It was the premier British royal garden to be involved in the French- and Dutch-inspired formalism that dominated for nearly a century, and it is entirely apt that today it is that period that has been so painstakingly and accurately preserved in the restoration.

LEFT
To the south of the palace William III's Great Fountain Garden has disappeared, but the patte d'oie *of avenues into the park survives as a grand layout.*

Het Loo

APELDOORN · THE NETHERLANDS

The significance and drama of Het Loo's story, for both royal and European garden design more generally, has been well summed up by the garden historian Jan van Asbeck: "No other historical garden has gained such international celebrity immediately after its construction (c.1693), vanished from the face of the earth after 115 years and finally, 175 years later, been restored in all its former glory as though time had stood still for the intervening three centuries." From its beginning Het Loo became the most ambitious and prestigious garden in the Netherlands, bringing together the influence of the Renaissance and French baroque gardens with the Dutch style in a manner achieved nowhere else. The decision at the end of the 1970s not only to restore the formal gardens but to do so with a painstaking eye for the original detail ensured that Het Loo regained its pre-eminent status.

In 1684 Prince William of Orange, Stadhouder of the Netherlands, purchased the medieval castle of Het Oude Loo, primarily as a hunting-lodge, but almost straight away it was

ABOVE
Fountains were always a major feature in the parterres at Het Loo, and the work carried out on them has ensured that they have been regained to their rightful status.

RIGHT
The garden's quantity of outstanding statuary, urns and vases, and other ornaments have benefited from expert attention in the restoration.

clear that he had ambitious plans for a new palace and the gardens. The work on both was carried out by Jacob Roman, who would later become William's official royal architect, and by Daniel Marot, a French Huguenot garden designer who had fled to Holland in 1685. In 1688 William and his English wife Mary were crowned King and Queen of England, and despite their long absences from Holland their new gardens at Het Loo were not neglected. On the contrary they were extended on a more ambitious scale than before.

The most important single factor influencing the 20th-century restoration was a detailed contemporary account from the late 17th century recorded by William's private physician, Dr Walter Harris, and published in London in 1699 under the title *A description of the King's Royal Palace and Gardens at Loo*. While the doctor's admiration for both the gardens and his royal master – as demonstrated in the first quotation below – are clear, it was the level of detail, both of

ABOVE
Looking across the Great Garden, the intricate arrangement of the design, planting, water and ornamental features have been minutely restored.

OPPOSITE
A detail from the swirling patterns of the parterre where planting and decorative stonework have been combined for effect.

the garden's proportions and layout and of the waterworks and ornamental details (in evidence in the second quotation) that would prove vital to the restoration. "The Gardens are most sumptuous and magnificent, adorned with greater variety of most noble *Fountains, Cascades, Parterres, Gravel Walks and Green Walks, Groves, Statues, Urns, Paintings*, and pleasant Prospects into the Country…a work of wonderful Magnificence, most worthy of so Great a Monarch…" He then states more specifically: "On the Terrestrial Globe the four parts of the world are exactly painted and out of the several parts of it there do spring a great number of sprouts, which throw up the water from all parts of it. On the other globe the twelve signs of the Zodiac are curiously painted the stars gilded and out of abundance of the stars there sprout out *jettes* on all sides."

By the time that Harris published his description the gardens were effectively complete, a baroque lay-out on a scale never attempted before or afterwards in Holland. The design of the garden closely followed Renaissance principles with a symmetry to the patterned beds, the inclusion of water features and ornament, and the sunken positioning of the gardens to maximize the effect of looking down onto them from raised terraces; this combined with the Dutch tradition of enclosure and a French magnificence of the overall effect. On either side of the new palace's flanking east and west wings were the King and Queen's gardens, overlooked by the respective royal apartments, as was the case at William and Mary's garden at Hampton Court. Although the designs in these two areas were intricate, both focusing on central fountain basins, they were modest in comparison with the other principle area of the Great Garden to the north, extending to some 6ha (15 acres) and enclosed on all sides. This was divided into the large rectangular Lower Garden closest to the palace, surrounded on three sides by raised terraces, and the Upper Garden. On the far side from the

palace a cross axis of avenues, leading in one direction west to the Het Oude Loo castle, divided the Lower Garden from the Upper Garden, with curving boundaries and terminating in central quarter-circle colonnades.

The Lower Garden was made up of eight symmetrical parterres (almost certainly designed by Marot), with a magnificent central fountain of Venus and tritons flanked by the two celestial and terrestrial globe fountains. The centrepiece of the Upper Garden was the octagonal fountain basin adorned with the king's fountain, which threw up a jet of water to a height of nearly 14m (46ft), and, being fed by an abundant local spring, played constantly with never any need to be turned off. These were the largest of the waterworks in the gardens, although one of the defining features of Het Loo was the manner in which the parterre design was enlivened by the number of fountains and cascades, in particular the Narcissus and Galatea cascades against the side terraces on the axis of the globes and Venus fountain. In all the gardens the ornamental detail was complemented by immaculately arranged and trained plants including clipped box, juniper, and hornbeam, and an array of flowering plants, many of which were carefully listed by Harris.

For late-17th-century visitors the pleasures of Het Loo were not limited to the main formal areas on three sides of the palace. On both sides of the Lower Garden was a series of enclosed gardens with different features such as an orangery or a maze. When the Englishman, Edward Southwell, visited in 1696 he recorded that in the area to one side of the Upper Garden, where six avenues radiated away, the outstanding feature was the large square *vivier* or reservoir, which he considered "One of the greatest beauties in the Garden".

During William and Mary's lifetime the gardens' reputation was immediate and remained untroubled through the 18th century. With the declaration of the Batavian Republic in 1795, however, Het Loo was abandoned, and the gardens partly plundered. By this time the beginning of a landscape park had been added, and when Het Loo came under the control of Napoleon's brother in 1807 the remaining formal gardens disappeared. Ornaments were broken or removed, the cascades dismantled, and over much of the site of the great baroque gardens Louis Napoleon had a picturesque landscape garden created. The Dutch royal family returned to Het Loo in 1813, but subsequent planting of trees and shrubberies during the 19th and 20th centuries further obscured the original gardens, while parts of the Queen's Garden disappeared under new extensions to the palace.

LEFT
Part of the glory of Het Loo derives from the combination of the palace, regimented formal gardens, and the surrounding woodland, as shown here.

It was following the death of Queen Wilhelmina, in 1975, that the decision was taken for Het Loo to formally become a state property and for a museum focusing on the Orange royal dynasty to be created in the palace. These changes initiated the decision for the gardens to be restored to the late-17th-century originals which, represented the outstanding gardening achievement of the royal family, both in the Netherlands and in England.

It is interesting that at the time a number of landscape gardeners in Holland and elsewhere were opposed to the removal of the landscape park to make way for a restored formal garden. Once the decision to proceed had been agreed, however, there were to be few compromises, only that the restoration would be confined to the main areas of the Great Garden and the King and Queen's gardens, the latter restricted by the fact that some of it had been covered by buildings, which would not be removed. The most complete restoration would be focused on the rectangular Lower Garden with its eight parterres, fountains, and cascades; the detailed restoration in the Upper Garden was restricted to four of the original eight parterres.

A combination of archaeology and contemporary descriptions and plans (as was the case at Hampton Court (*see pp. 138–43*)) provided the detailed framework for the restoration. In Het Loo's case the principle source of information was Harris's description, and the details he provided, both of ornaments and the plants used in the parterres, has allowed for a remarkable degree of historical accuracy. In addition to the clipped box and other hedging and topiary materials the flowering plants used have been restricted to varieties known to have flourished in the 17th century.

LEFT
Much of the garden's original character has been given back by the return of the various shades and shapes of clipped evergreens, including box and yew.

ABOVE
Arched bowers and walkways shaded by trained plants were a favoured feature in the original King and Queen's gardens on either side of the palace.

If the most subtle details of the restoration have been effected in the planting, the most striking are in the various ornaments. A search resulted in a number of original statues being returned from other gardens where they had ended up. While these statues usually required extensive restoration, in some cases fragments found in the gardens during the archaeological stage enabled replicas to be made. A few important items, such as the Narcissus Cascade, had been given to museums, and copies of these had to be made from scratch. But most significant has been the recreation of the original decorative scheme composed by statues and other ornaments.

More than anything however, it is the rediscovered balance of overall scale and symmetrically harmonious detail – of plants, ornaments, water, and perhaps most crucial, spatial alignment – that is the restoration's principle achievement. The way in which the gardens revolve around the palace building and link one area to another, via steps or terraced walks, illustrates the orderliness that was an unchallenged requirement of European gardens in the 17th century. In royal gardens it had the added significance of reflecting their status, something that would not have been lost on the ambitious Prince William of Orange.

Restored gardens have been written off as dull and unoriginal, pastiches with little authenticity. The work at Het Loo counters any such argument and confirms the satisfaction to be derived from the restoration of such an historically significant garden. The achievement is illustrated by comparing the aerial photograph above with the contemporary engraving taken from a similarly elevated viewpoint opposite. The scale, detail, and symmetrical arrangement are virtually reproduced, and it is remarkable that three centruies separate the two views. Both images confirm the particular Dutch characteristic of the gardens compared to the earlier great formal styles of France and Italy; the expansion of a detailed geometric pattern over a predominantly horizontal plane and always in close harmony with the focal point of the palace building.

The new plants in the restored garden and the immaculate edges to the topiary and low hedges reveal how important such orderliness was to the orginal picture. It is only since the restoration that the combined effect of the different patterns has once again been revealed. Wherever you are in the gardens, different parts of features can be taken individually, whether a statue or other ornament, a section of parterre, or the vista of a path. But the importance of the garden, and what so faithfully recreates the appearance and mood of the original period, is the manner in which the component parts all flow seamlessly together. With the return of the overall grand scheme the iconography of the gardens, presented by the positioning of statues and other ornaments and the manner in which they lead one from another, is once again clear and demonstrates that however horticulturally advanced, gardens of the late 17th and early 18th centuries always had a non-horticultural message. There is, however, also continuity in the plants. In early summer the parterres are ablaze with luxurious striped 'Rembrandt' tulips. These and other parrot tulips were grown in the original gardens as showpieces at a time when they were exotic luxuries available only to the most privileged gardeners. The records confirm that William's wife, Mary, had a collection of primulas in the orangery, and these are among the plants that have been put back into the gardens. When William and Mary were making and then enjoying Het Loo, there was a strong priority that the gardens were seen to be glorifying the House of Orange, demonstrating its secure establishment and its artistic good taste.

Today the links with the Royal House of Orange remain strong, as demonstrated by displays in the garden during the early summer of 2005, to celebrate the Silver Jubilee of Queen Beatrix; these included a number of tulips, such as 'Princess Beatrix', named after different members of the royal family and other plants that alluded to the dynasty. They are examples of how these gardens are far from being a pastiche of the original; by skilful research and archaeology an extraordinary degree of accuracy was attained and this laid the foundations for the gardens to enjoy a new renaissance.

LEFT
This aerial view demonstrates the vast overall scale of Het Loo and the immaculate design of the palace and gardens.

RIGHT
A contemporary engraving of Het Loo in the bird's-eye style that was popular at the end of the 17th century. It shows the relationship between palace and gardens.

Isola Bella

LAKE MAGGIORE · ITALY

The garden of Isola Bella has been one of the most admired of all Italian gardens ever since it was begun for Count Carlo Borromeo *c.*1630. Since its creation it has remained in the hands of the same family and today is the home of Prince Borromeo-Arese. Count Carlo began the transformation of a rocky island on Lake Maggiore with a palace and terraced gardens that cover the whole area. His work was continued by his son and by the end of the 17th century Isola Bella was perhaps the most unique Italian baroque garden. The drama of the island setting with views across the lake to the Alps is matched by the design of terraces and the decoration with ornaments such as statues mounted on dizzy pedestals and towering obelisks.

Count Carlo's plan was extraordinarily ambitious, for at the time the island was bare with rocky edges dropping away into steep cliffs to the sea. The setting was matched for audacity by the proposed design originally drawn up by Angelo Crivelli, to create a picture of a huge galleon sailing across the lake. The construction took many years and was continued by Count Carlo's son, Count Vitaliano, but even by 1685 an early visitor, Bishop Gilbert Burnet, was describing it

OPPOSITE
The symmetry of clipped trees contrasts characteristically with brilliant climbers against the walls. From everywhere there are views across the lake to hills in the distance.

BELOW
Looking from the lake to Isola Bella's theatrical terraces, whose ingenious design is as spellbinding today as it was over three centuries ago when the palace was built.

as: "One of the liveliest spots of ground in the World." A number of engravings, mostly executed during the 18th century, all emphasize the appearance of a galleon, with the palace towards the "prow" and theatre and garden terraces forming the "stern". The effect was added to by the ornamental decoration as Geoffrey Jellicoe has described: "The terraces bristle with sculpture whose silhouette is suggestive of masts and spars."

The sculptural ornament does not only contribute to the appearance of a galleon, it is positioned for maximum effect on the corners of the terraces' retaining walls, always raised up on plinths and in other places on lofty columns to create a series of dramatic silhouettes. The impression is most dramatic from the upper levels when the descending terraces and figures are set against the deep blue background of the lake. The sense of movement in the garden's design triumphantly achieved one of the key components of gardens of the Italian Renaissance. In fact, given the date of Isola Bella and the theatrical richness of ornamental decoration is theatrical in some places – for instance the ampitheatre, where an array of statues and obelisks topped by a unicorn (the symbol of the Borromeo family) have often led to it being referred to as rococo. This is exemplified in the subterranean grottoes through which parts of the garden are accessible from the palace, as well as the grotto-like recesses with shells and water features.

There was evidence of planting in the gardens by the mid-18th century, in the descriptions of visitors, but today the restored planting by Prince Borromeo-Arese has brought the terraces to life in a manner not achieved since the original construction. When he succeeded to the ownership of the island, the statues and other ornament and the strong lines of the terraces dominated the scene. Now, the striking combination of planting and architecture gives the garden an added dimension. In some instances the planting complements the formality, in the swirling patterns of low-clipped hedges and annuals planted by colour in the parterre below the theatre, or in the rows of evergreens clipped into globes lining the terrace paths. In others, however, the colour or form of plants provides a brilliant foil, with cascades of colourful climbers and wall plants tumbling off the stone masonry, the contrast of clipped box and brilliant flowers in terracotta pots flanking flights of steps or decorating terrace balustrades, and all softening the stone-work and architecture.

Much of the planting that has been done in recent years takes advantage of the island's climate, and rare and tender exotics abound. Numerous terracotta pots contain lemon trees and orange trees are espaliered against sheltered walls. One path has been transformed into a walk of pomegranates, and elsewhere there are myrtles, magnolias, and camphor trees. The impact of the planting is often maximized by the repeated use of single colours, not only in the beds of the parterre but in rows of pots or long narrow borders beneath retaining walls. Other subtle touches include a massed planting of lily-of-the-valley beneath the rows of pomegranate trees and the tender climbing fig, *Ficus pumila*, which spreads its foliage across large areas of the walls.

Nearly four centuries after Isola Bella was begun it has lost none of its sparkling originality, both in decoration and construction – one of the twin hexagonal pavilions that flank the terraces, when looking from the parterre, still conceals the pumping equipment that was installed in the original garden to pump water from the lake to the holding cistern on an upper terrace from where it is distributed through the gardens. In recent years the garden has gained an array of flowering decoration that greatly enhances the overall effect and, at the same time, creates a veneer of immaculate presentation that impresses all visitors. For most, however, it only adds to the abiding memory of statues silhouetted against the lake, or the view on a crisp early morning to the distant snow-covered peaks of the Alps.

LEFT
An 18th-century engraving of the terraced gardens at one end of the island confirms how the original design was strongly architectural.

BELOW
Looking down onto the immaculately restored patterns of the parterre below the terraces, a rare balance of innovative planting and ornament.

RIGHT
The narrow intimacy of steps leading to a side walk along one of the terraces contrasts with the lofty statue and obelisks in the background.

Charlottenburg

BERLIN · GERMANY

Many consider Charlottenburg, with the oldest garden in Berlin, to be Germany's most impressive baroque palace and garden composition, but it only survives today thanks to painstaking restoration following devastation of both palace and garden during World War II – inevitable given its position just west of the city centre. The harmony of architecture and formal garden design is as complete as in any garden of the period, and the detail of the restoration work extends to the buildings as well as the main area of the garden.

Although begun a few years earlier, Charlottenburg fittingly celebrated the crowning of the Elector Frederick III of Brandenburg as the first King of Prussia, in 1701, an elevation that was to have a powerful influence through Germany for over two centuries. But at the same time as providing an outlet for the new king's extravagant love of grandeur – evident in the enormous palace with its lofty central dome, which was begun in 1695 – Charlottenburg

OPPOSITE
One of the superb buildings added to the landscape garden to one side of the main parterre at the end of the 18th century and, like the palace, restored after World War II.

BELOW
Looking across the parterre, whose wide horizontal design accentuates the impact of the building's façade and towering central dome.

provided an opening for an already distinguished royal gardening dynasty. Frederick's wife was Sophie Charlotte, daughter of the Electress Sophie of Hanover and sister of King George I of England, who had only a few years previously created the celebrated *Grosser Garten* at the Dukes and Electors' summer residence of Herrenhausen. Like her mother, Sophie Charlotte was cultured and artistic; she was known as "the philosophical queen". The garden at Charlottenburg was primarily created under her instructions, by her gardener, the Frenchman Siméon Godeau, who had studied under André Le Nôtre. It has been argued that Le Nôtre himself supplied an original design for the garden in 1696, although it was rejected by Sophie Charlotte as too simple.

The overriding features of the garden are the enormous rectangular parterre, which, in both scale and intricacy of design, matches the main palace building from where it stretches out centrally, and the use of water from the River Spree, which extends along one side of the garden and curves around beyond the far end of the parterre. The ample supply of water allowed for the creation of an enormous formal *bassin* between the parterre and the river, further enhancing the scale of the overall picture, and the presence of the waters of the Spree bordering the garden on two sides gave an element of

BELOW
The enormous restored parterre stretching away from the palace to the main pool at the far end. The flanking woodlands enhance the scale of the overall picture.

BELOW RIGHT
An engraving of the palace and early garden clearly showing the River Spree along the right side and curving round at the far end.

Dutch formality in addition to the French-inspired grandeur. Significantly, the parterre was not enlivened by numerous fountains, although that would have been very easy. Instead, the patterns of *tapis verts* were decorated with outstanding statuary, in particular a rare set of marble figures of twelve Roman emperors.

The ruinously extravagant King Frederick extended the overall size of the gardens more than once, and there were unexecuted plans for it to be increased even further, taking in areas beyond the quadruple avenues that lined the parterre and the woods behind, or on either side of the main central vista beyond the River Spree. But after his death in 1713 few changes were made for most of the 18th century as his son Frederick William I was not a gardening enthusiast, and his grandson, Frederick the Great, preferred Sanssouci (*see pp. 50–5*). Towards the end of the 18th century significant additions were made by Frederick William II, which were continued by his son, Frederick William III, notably the addition of two memorable garden buildings, the Mausoleum and the Neuer Pavilion.

As happened in other German gardens at the time, the landscape garden proved a powerful influence over much of Charlottenburg. Frederick William II employed Johann August Eyserbeck and Peter Josef Lenné, who naturalized the formal *bassin* in the central design into a lake and dramatically rearranged the parterres to soften the rigid symmetry. He also commissioned the Belvedere building, later referred to as the Belvedere tea house, which was designed by Carl Gotthard Langhams in the area of the park that Eyserbeck created to one side of the central parterre. In 1810 Frederick William III commissioned the Mausoleum as the burial place of his wife, Queen Luise; this was designed by Heinrich Gentz in collaboration with Karl Friedrich Schinkel, as a Doric temple. It was also the burial place for Frederick William III himself, Kaiser William I, Kaiserin Augusta, and Princess Liegnitz. Schinkel was one of the most-admired German architects and landscape designers of the 19th century and he also designed the other outstanding building that Frederick William III commissioned as a small residential house, called the Neuer Pavilion, although now often known as the Schinkel Pavilion.

From 1943 the palace and gardens suffered grevious wartime damage, and much of it was left unrecognizable. It is to the credit of the German authorities during the 1950s that Charlottenburg was one of the royal palaces and gardens where restoration was carried out to the highest standard. Today it has regained the landscape and ornamental quality of its original heyday, shortly after its creation.

Beloeil

BRUSSELS · BELGIUM

OPPOSITE
*A view across the great
basin that encapsulates
the qualities of Beloeil –
a simple combination of
water, architecture, trees,
and limited ornament
on an impressive scale.*

Garden restoration takes various forms, from drastic reconstruction to more subtle renovation. The latter restores a garden's appearance – and with it the atmosphere – without imposing a veneer of newness that comes with gleaming restored statuary and small immaculate new plants. Beloeil, the outstanding French-style landscape in Belgium belongs to the latter group and, after sensitive work by the present owner, Antoine, the 13th Prince de Ligne, has regained the splendour of the 18th century when the garden of Beloeil was first created.

The royal princes of Ligne have owned the property since 1511, but the present château, on which the landscape focuses, was built during the 17th century by Prince Claude-Lamoral de Ligne. His grandson, Prince Claude-Lamoral II, created the garden during the mid-18th century with the help of two architects, Jean-Baptiste Bergé and Jean Michel Chevotet. The prince's ambitious plan centred on the enormous formal basin covering nearly 6ha (15 acres), which the château overlooks, and which dominates the whole landscape by virtue of its sheer size. A long, broad rectangle of water extends away from the château terrace and terminates in fitting style at the far end with a spectacular fountain group of Neptune with attendant sea horses and tritons, made by Adrien Henrion, a pupil of the French master-sculptor, Jean–Baptiste Pigalle.

The scale of the basin makes a superb contrast to the areas of garden that lie concealed on both sides. They form a pair of parallel axes, separated from the central basin by long beech avenues, which Philip Mansel, the biographer of Prince Charles-Joseph de Ligne, describes as being like "an enfilade of antechambers in an 18th-century palace, one room opens onto the next in a straight line". They are of the utmost simplicity with areas of grass, many focusing on pools that are linked together by small streams, and enclosed by clipped hornbeam hedges, beech and hornbeam trees, and pleached limes.

It seems quite likely that the flamboyant names given to the various enclosures or *bosquets* originate from the period of Prince Claude-Lamoral II's son, Prince Charles-Joseph, a diplomat, soldier, and writer. He was an immensely cheerful character who lit up the courts of late-18th century Europe and shared his father's enjoyment of gardens and Beloeil. Three of the enclosures are *Le Rieu d'Amour*, *Le Bassin des Poisons Rouges*, and *La Sale du Grand Diable*, named after an early ancestor, Prince Antoine I. One, *Le Boulingrin*, was an outdoor theatre where plays were staged. Prince Charles-Joseph extended the gardens with an English-style landscape called

the Deer Park to the east of the château, and decorated this with a series of buildings – a Modavian temple, a Gothic ruin, and an obelisk in memory of his son, who died a soldier. He also entertained in spectacular style, holding regular fêtes, which were attended by hundreds of guests, and involved boating on the *basin*, and fireworks. After one he recorded that there were "eight or 10,000 dancers, masked or not masked as they wished, barrels of apricot juice and lemonade, mountains of apples and oranges, and much procreation".

Among his many books ranging from history to poetry Prince Charles-Joseph wrote one celebrating European gardening taste of the 18th century, entitled, *Coup d'oeil sur Beloeil et sur une grande partie des jardins de l'Europe*, and originally published privately. As well as enthusing about the different styles of garden design that emerged during the 18th century, whether French formality or the English landscape, Prince Charles-Joseph constantly urges his readers to relax in

ABOVE
Looking along one of the many canals in the gardens on either side of the basin, flanked by tall hedges that have been carefully retrained and clipped to the desired height.

RIGHT
In another area an ingenious natural clipped pergola surrounds a formal pool and demonstrates yet another ingenious combination of foliage and water.

gardening, as, for example, in the following passage: "Love of the countryside increases with age, inspires, fulfils, consoles and makes life worth living. The secret of life is to plant with flowers the short distance that separates the cradle of infancy from the sanctuary of death."

In 1900 the central block of the château was destroyed by fire, and only the wings remained. The family rebuilt it in a style faithful to the original but later in the 20th century the gardens suffered serious damage as a result of occupation during both world wars. Since then the present owner, Prince Antoine de Ligne, has carried out dedicated restoration, which has returned the orderliness needed for the long axes and symmetrical design to achieve their full effect. Overgrown trees have been trimmed back, old and decaying ones replaced with young specimens that have been trained and clipped to the required height. This was the case in one enclosure, named the Ladies Pond because here female guests bathed in privacy during the 18th century. All the hornbeams that surrounded it were either decaying or too big and out of shape to take in hand, so Prince Antoine replaced them with new ones, which

have been trained to a uniform height of 7m (23ft). In one walk, called the *Miroirs* or Mirrors, the lines of hornbeams on either side have been trained to a height that is exactly two-thirds the width of the walk, in accordance with the suggestions set out by the 18th-century French scientific writer Antoine-Joseph Dezalier d'Argenville, whose publication *Traité sur la théorie et la practique de jardinage*, celebrated the garden designs of Le Nôtre.

Other enclosures or long axial vistas include one of the few areas given over to flowering plants, the Rose Garden named in honour of the roses planted here centuries ago that were among the first in Belgium, and the *Allée du Doyen* which stretches for 600m (1,968ft) between rows of now towering hornbeams linked at the top by arches over which they are trained. The Quincunx is surrounded by copper beeches that were planted *c*.1950 to replace ordinary beech trees that had been blown down in a great storm in 1942. Whether the Children's Playground or the Cloister, the names of most of the enclosures are the charming originals that were given to them in the 18th century.

In the 1720s Prince Claude-Lamoral originally laid out the formal potager to the east of the château, and the restoration has ensured that it remains there today, decorated in the centre by the Temple of Pomona that was added by Prince Charles-Joseph. It was designed for him by the French architect François-Joseph Belanger, who was also responsible for the buildings that decorate the Deer Park: the obelisk in memory of the prince's son, the Ruin, the Temple of Morpheus, and the summerhouse built on the Island of Flora.

Today the gardens have evolved into a state of wonderful maturity enhanced by sympathetic maintenance. (Perhaps most challenging is the clipping required by 10km (6¼ miles) of hedges.) The gentle curves to the edges of the main lake, the rectangular vegetable gardens, and the sense of establishment, together with the simple combination of water, open space, and light filtering through the foliage – which takes on subtly changing hues through the seasons from fresh pale green in spring to rich autumn gold – gives the garden an atmosphere that visitors cannot fail to enjoy.

The different tastes of successive royal generations have all been allowed to leave their mark on the initial grand creation over three centuries ago, ensuring that today the effect is more enjoyable than ever. One contemporary visitor's description captures the spirit of the garden as it is today and confirms that one of its most enduring qualities is that its essence is the same as when it was originally designed in the 18th century.

"Beloeil is a great stretch of water like a mirror to the heavens – a mirror with a frame round it. Be silent and look. The clouds can be seen reflected and they twist and turn in the water just as they do in the sky. The sun plays with the shadow it makes. The lime-trees pruned to form continuous screens and the fences of hornbeams with their opaque portions and the gaps between them leave it to the sun to give them such mobility as they have; the sun moves round and rises high in the sky at noon before descending again by the evening so that it is first to be seen on the left, then opposite and then on the right…Beloeil is a great sight but not a spectacular one. It has a solid presence, with no ragged edges but with no fancy flourishes."

Today these exact same qualities of contrasting intimacy and spaciousness, the extraordinary effect of the great expanse of water, and the almost total colour predominance of monochrome green, continue to hold visitors spellbound. There is a simplicity at Beloeil, despite the overall scale and the size of the château, which makes this a garden with an intensely philosophical message. Visitors do not come here to admire flowers or other plants, or to wonder at impressive ornaments. Instead, they come to enjoy a certain mood and to reflect on the garden's continuity through successive centuries. That they might not recognize the restoration that has been carried out in recent decades is testament to the quality and subtlety of the work.

FROM GRANDEUR
TO PRIVACY

THREE CENTURIES AGO MANY royal gardens were created to show off, to demonstrate power, patronage, taste, and wealth. Today, while many are only possible because of considerable wealth, they fulfil a different function for their owners – the provision of privacy. Members of royal families are by default public figures, and the modern media has greatly increased their exposure. Surviving royal families no longer rule their countries but they do lead lives busy with public duties. In this light, privacy has become increasingly important to them, and it is best enjoyed in their own homes and gardens.

Queen Victoria opened the doors to the public at Hampton Court as early as 1838, but by then the royal family was no longer using the palace as a residence. Nowadays a royal residence that is not the private property of the royal family will almost certainly be open to the public to some extent. To balance this there will be periods when the gardens of an official residence are closed to the public, as in the case at Fredensborg in Denmark where this arrangement allows the royal family to continue to use the family's favourite home. A great many palaces are no longer used as royal residences, and some of these are discussed in other chapters.

Some places, however, were always intended to be private, often situated in remote positions such as Balchik in Bulgaria and the Castle of Mey in Scotland. Both the homes of royal ladies, they retain an air of intimacy and seclusion. They also reflect the personal tastes of their creators and the features they most enjoyed, whether ornamental or in the planting, and these are carefully preserved for posterity. The fact that Balchik is now part of the Sofia University Botanic Garden has not intruded into the garden's atmosphere, and, in the same way, the trust that took on the ownership of the Castle of Mey in 2002 will ensure that the character of the castle and its garden is well preserved.

Today it is in their private gardens, rather than in their offical residences, that members of royal families can indulge a love of gardening and create something that reflects their personal taste, and this is particularly evident at the gardens of Highgrove in England and Belvédère (*see pp. 126–33*) in Belgium. Here are gardens of devoted enthusiasts, who have combined originality with a quality of design and thoughtful planting that bears comparison to the best of their contemporaries. These gardens pay great attention to detail and continue the tradition of excellent quality that has characterized royal gardens in Europe for centuries.

Highgrove and Belvédère confirm what has always been the case, that where individual members of royal families have an interest in gardening they will take advantage of the resources at their disposal to create something with high standards and lasting interest. Some of the gardens discussed in earlier chapters of this book did not come about primarily because of the gardening enthusiasm of their owners, but to make a statement and create a visible show of royal taste and

LEFT
Fredericksburg Castle in Denmark, superbly impressive but in recent decades retained primarily as a state palace rather than a private home as with nearby Fredensborg.

RIGHT
The combination of exotic foliage, ornamental statuary, and the pattern of ironwork and glass is a fundamental element to the glasshouses at Laeken in Belgium.

PREVIOUS PAGES
The mysterious and private pool near the Stumpery in the woodland garden at Highgrove, in England, is one of the many individual areas in the garden.

patronage. But at the same time an interest in gardening has been constantly evident in all periods, and has resulted in some of the most inspired and enjoyable gardens. There is no doubt that the trend is evident today and will carry on in the future, as along as the royal families continue to reign.

Taken as a group, the contribution of these places to European garden history is immense; looked at individually an extraordinary cross-section of gardening taste and style is evident. They produce a roll call of some of some of the most distinguished designers, craftsmen, and horticulturalists in successive periods and contribute in all areas of gardening from architectural to botanical. Without such a rich source of opportunity it could be argued that the achievements and reputations of many of these people would not have been so substantial, but evidence of their work can still be admired to a remarkably high degree.

Fredensborg Palace

LAKE ESRUM · DENMARK

King Frederick IV decided to build a new palace called Fredensborg to celebrate the end of the Northern War against Charles II of Sweden in 1720. After having been humiliated in the early years of the war, his country came out of it with more respect. Fredensborg means "castle of peace", and before the transformation of his fortunes in war Frederick had already come to love the remote estate bordering Lake Esrum in the North Sealand, which his father Christian V had acquired for hunting in 1678. This affection has been retained ever since, and in an instance of remarkable continuity Fredensborg has been the Danish royal family's favourite residence for most periods since it was built. Today it provides an ideal example of the balance between a state treasure accessible to the public, and a private royal residence, which it is for the seasons of spring and autumn for Queen Margrethe II and her husband Prince Henrik.

Frederick IV was fortunate in having a highly talented gardener, Johan Cornelius Krieger, who designed the palace and laid out the gardens. Krieger's palace was a small domed

RIGHT
An early gouache view of Fredensborg by an unknown artist. The painting emphasizes the domesticity of the buildings in front of the main palace with its distinctive dome.

BELOW
An aerial view showing the distinctive octagonal court, the patte d'oie of avenues, and Lake Esrum beyond, as well as the Marble Garden and other formal areas to the left.

main building, with a highly original octagonal court in front that was enclosed by single-storey buildings containing servants' quarters. There was also the orangery, chapel, and stables. Through the 18th century the main palace underwent steady alteration, which included raising it by one storey and adding the four corner pavilions.

Krieger's garden was in part assisted by the existing hunting paths, but the bold design linked it immediately to the formal French style still pre-eminent in Europe at the beginning of the 18th century. In front of the palace a *patte d'oie* of seven avenues was laid out around a semicircle focusing on a similarly semicircular parterre in front of the main building. *Bosquets* of young woodland were planted between the avenues, some with magnificent views to the lake, which curves round to form the boundary to the landscape in front of the palace and along one side.

Krieger's gardens were developed under Frederick IV's grandson, Frederick VI, who employed Nicolas Henry Jardin, a French designer who emphasized the French-inspired

formality of the original design. He created the broad *tapis-vert* flanked by double avenues of trees, which accentuated the perspective of the main vista. Further additions were made later in the 18th century, notably the work of the neoclassical sculptor Johannes Wiedewelt, whose sculptures add distinctive ornament to the gardens. To the west of the palace one avenue through the woods, the *Konge Alle*, leads to perhaps Fredensborg's most individual area, the *Nordmandsdalen* or Norman Valley. Here are a collection of sixty stone figures by the sculptor J.G. Grund, depicting peasants, fisherman, farmers, and their women from the northern parts of the kingdom, Norway and the Faroes.

As the gardens matured they were in part converted to a romantic landscape style, which saw some of the straight formal vistas becoming winding paths through the woodland. For the royal family an Indian summer of social life came towards the end of the 19th century during the reign of Christian IX and Queen Louise, known in Denmark as the Fredensborg days. They were sometimes called "the grandparents of Europe" and regularly gathered together groups of different members of Europe's royal families. Their daughter Alexandra married the English Prince of Wales and later became Queen Alexandra; her younger sister, Dagmar, married Alexander III of Russia and was the mother of the last Russian tsar, Nicholas II.

Ever since that period Fredensborg has been the favourite home of the royal family, and the gardens have benefited from constant attention. From the 1970s the formal lines of the main avenues were re-established with the planting of new trees, and the harmony between the limes of the avenues and the beeches that populate much of the woodland in the areas in between is one of the garden's most memorable features. Many of the original 18th-century features such as the figures in the *Nordmandsdalen* and the two summerhouses on the edge of the garden overlooking the lake survived, while others such

as a circular dell enclosed by pollarded limes have been painstakingly restored. Two of the most monumental sculpture groups by Wiedewelt, celebrating the twin countries of the old kingdom, Denmark and Norway, stand on either side of the entrance to the main central avenue, along which symmetrically arranged statues are lined on pedestals.

The combination of spaciousness, long avenues, and sculptural ornament ensures that the gardens retain the impressive baroque character that Frederick IV intended when he first created them. Indeed, the restoration of recent decades has returned the neatness and geometry of design that such a formal layout requires for full effect and which had been absent during years of over-maturity. An altogether more vibrant note is struck in the large enclosed *Marmorhave*, or Marble Garden, which lies to the west of the palace. Usually reserved as a private retreat for the royal family, it is open to the

public for the month of July, when visitors can enjoy the feast of flower and vegetable gardens. The *Marmorhave* was added as part of the 18th-century work by Jardin and Wiedewelt, and the latter's sculptures add to the richness of the floral displays. A succession of rose arches spreads across the main paths, lined by immaculate clipped hedges of dwarf boxes, and much of the main area is filled with symmetrical displays of fruit and vegetables. Along one side the garden is overlooked by Fredensborg's most recent architectural addition, a new orangery to make up for the loss of the original, which was transformed into living quarters during the 18th century. The new building was designed by Soren D. Schmidt in 1995 and is filled with plants, some rare and unusual, many arranged in decorative terracotta pots.

Frederick IV did not expand Fredensborg primarily for show, as was the case with other royal European gardens of his period. But he was well aware that the expansion of this home from a modest hunting lodge in idyllic natural surroundings to an extensive baroque palace with the relevant attendant buildings and formal gardens to complement the architecture, would confirm his appreciation of the French style and, therefore, his good taste. After some decades of little use during

ABOVE
Figures sculpted by Grund in the Nordmandsdalen *or* Norman Valley *are a rare example of sculpture celebrating ordinary working people of the time.*

OPPOSITE
Neatly patterned planting announces the entrance to the main avenue. The monuments to Denmark and Norway are positioned on either side.

the early 19th century, it later developed because its idyllic position made it certain to become a favourite royal home, which it has remained ever since. For Frederick IV it provided welcome privacy, when, after the death of his first wife, Queen Louise, he married his mistress of many years and elevated her to being queen – a move disapproved of by many of his people.

For more recent generations the abiding popularity of Fredensborg confirms the continuing importance of country life and country homes in Denmark. Queen Margrethe's annual stays at Fredensborg combine with the two seasons when the gardens and countryside are at their best: in spring and autumn. And at other times public visitors are able to share the enjoyment, admire the immaculate detail of the gardens, and look back to the history of the past three centuries.

Indeed, in many ways Fredensborg enjoys an arrangement that only survives in very few royal European gardens today, where it combines being a place of huge popularity and significance for the thousands of visitors who come every year,

with being the favourite home of the Danish royal family. As a result the gardens enjoy a higher standard of maintenance than at any time since they were originally laid out. The combination of the 18th-century formal features with the contemporary planting and architecture in the Marble Garden shows how continuity can bring harmonious development and ensure that gardens continue to evolve from one generation to another. Today the historic grandeur of the French-inspired original has been softened by the planting in the Marble Garden – something that fits into the overall formality and yet brings a contemporary feel and a more accessible scale. As at nearby Drottningholm (*see pp.56–61*) across the sea in Stockholm, what was created as a garden of statement has matured into somewhere entirely suitable for the combined demands of public access and royal privacy that needs to be sustained. Restoration has gone hand in hand with sympathetic new development, and the result is enjoyed by visitors all year round.

LEFT
The new orangery designed by Schmidt, which opened in 1995, has an impressive display of plants for most of the year.

BELOW
Regimented rows of vegetables enhance the impression of ornamental planting in the Marmorhave, which is overlooked by the orangery on the far side.

LEFT
One of the paths that divides the plots of the Marmorhave, or Marble Garden, covered in a succession of rose arches with box-edged beds of flowers and vegetables on both sides.

Balchik

BALCHIK · BULGARIA

Balchik, the most easterly garden featured in this book, and overlooking the shores of the Black Sea, remains an extraordinary period piece representing a brief haven during the turbulent affairs of the Balkans region, which was racked by wars and uprisings for centuries. As a result of the Second Balkan War, in 1913, Bulgaria was forced to cede the coastal strip of land adjoining the Black Sea known as South Dobruja to neighbouring Rumania, and it was during the period of Rumanian ownership that the small palace and its terraced gardens were created. But in 1940, Rumania (which had declared itself neutral in the struggles for power at the beginning of World War II) was forced by German-backed Bulgaria to return South Dobruja, and the territory has remained Bulgarian ever since. In 1955 the gardens became part of the Botanical Gardens of Sofia University.

The palace and garden was created by an English princess, granddaughter of both Queen Victoria and Tsar Alexander II – an intriguing reflection of how the dynastic tentacles of royal families spread throughout Europe during the 19th and early

OPPOSITE
Looking from one of the many terraces in the garden to the eclectic architecture of the small palace. The bedroom balcony confirms the benign climate.

BELOW
Both palace and garden architecture reveal a rich mixture of styles, as seen in the loggia with its elegant Oriental arches at the end of one terrace.

instability continued throughout the rest of Marie's life and beyond. A renowned beauty, Marie was clearly resourceful. Despite the remoteness of her home, she employed a fashionable French architect and garden designer to carry out the work and she showed a lifelong love of all things French.

The French journalist, Philippe Millet, wrote of her at the age of 50: "As she enters a room she seems at first glance to dominate all those present. She receives their homage as a sovereign should and has the air of reigning even when she says 'good day'. The chair on which she sits immediately becomes a throne."

The result of her efforts at Balchik bears all the hallmarks of the architectural style so popular in gardens of the 1920s and 1930s. The dramatic terraces, designed to take maximum advantage of the views over the Black Sea, arched loggias, and exotic planting form a picture comparable to the gardens being created in similar surroundings along the fashionable south of France coastline of the Côte d'Azur. The area of Rumania and Bulgaria had been a cultural melting pot for centuries, and different influences were incorporated into the garden's design and features, including Bulgarian, Moldavian, Mauritanian, and Oriental. The atmosphere that Queen Marie wanted to create is well illustrated by the name given to the palace by the locals, *Tenha Vuva* in Rumanian, meaning Quiet Nest. Under one of the garden's many rare trees is a stone throne on which the queen apparently sat in the evening to watch the sun setting over the water.

But as well as the tranquillity that the palace and garden provided for Marie, it was her interest in botany and the unusual species that flourish in the coastal climate that played a part in securing Balchik's future after her death. In the Stalinist Bulgaria of the 1950s the preservation of an old Rumanian royalist haven would have been unlikely, but the educational value of the garden to the country's main university in Sofia allowed Balchik to survive. Marie planted the majority of the estimated 3000 different plant species in the gardens today (many rare and exotic), including a large number of the 200 or so different trees. Today, with the air full of the scent of roses and jasmine tumbling from the walls, brilliant flowering and fruiting plants such as magnolias and pomegranates, and the cool water in cascades and canals, Balchik retains an air of enchantment that Queen Marie instilled with her creation of a private seaside haven.

In some ways, notably in the architecture of the palace and the garden's terraces and buildings, it is very much a period piece, a product of a time when such chic seaside retreats, whether here or in other parts of Europe, were the height of fashion. But the quality of the plants and trees, and the fact that it is now part of a botanic garden, gives Balchik a rare degree of horticultural interest. It is a reminder of a bygone age in European royal history, but one that survives with far more than just nostalgia.

20th centuries. Princess Marie was the daughter of Victoria's second son, Prince Alfred, who became Duke of Edinburgh and Saxe-Coburg-Gotha, and his wife, Grand Duchess Marie Alexandrovna, the tsar's only daughter. In 1893 Princess Marie married her cousin, the Prussian Prince Ferdinand, who was designated by the German powers to be the successor to the heirless King Carol I of Rumania. So on Carol's death in 1914, Ferdinand succeeded as king. He remained king of Rumania through the upheavals of World War I until his death in 1927. A few years before, in 1924, Queen Marie had begun to create the summer palace and its gardens; this would remain her home until her death in 1938.

Reading the vicissitudes of Rumanian affairs at the time, it is clear that from the death of her husband Marie's home and garden at Balchik were an escape and respite from the unsettled state of the nation's affairs in which her family was centrally involved. She herself had played a major part while her husband was alive and yet could only watch as the events of the ensuing years unfolded. Her son, Carol, initially renounced his claim to the throne; then, a few years after his father Ferdinand's death, when his own son Michael had been crowned king, he changed his mind, forced his son off the throne and installed himself. But by now this tyrannical monarchy was becoming increasingly unpopular, and its

OPPOSITE
The palace's dramatic position is confirmed by this picture, which looks down to a formal pool surrounded by clipped evergreens and the sea just beyond.

RIGHT
The marriage of architecture and planting is entirely apt for the exotic climate, as can be seen here with the climbers draping much of the stonework.

BELOW
The view out over the Black Sea was the primary reason for the palace's position, and today, looking out across the garden's flowerbeds, it is easy to see why.

Castle of Mey

CAITHNESS · SCOTLAND

The search for privacy might not have been the primary incentive for the late Queen Elizabeth the Queen Mother to purchase the Castle of Mey, but its remote position on the far northern shore of Scotland guaranteed it. And it was, certainly in the early years, as an escape that Mey appealed to the Queen Mother. She first saw it when she was coming to terms with the sudden death of her husband, King George VI, in 1952. She was staying nearby with friends, who suggested they might take a picnic to the old deserted castle at Mey as they understood it was for sale. By this time renamed Barrogill Castle and unoccupied for years, it was in a sad state, but three months later it was in the ownership of the Queen Mother. As she said some years afterwards, "I found the Castle of Mey, with its long history, its serene beauty and its proud setting, faced with the prospect of having no one to occupy it. I felt a great wish to preserve, if I could, this ancient dwelling."

RIGHT

The castle's fairytale-like turrets provide the focal point for all parts of the gardens. Here on the east, the yellow Primula florindae *flourishes.*

OPPOSITE

Looking down into a corner of the walled garden, with the delightful tower and display greenhouses as well as a cornucopia of beds protected by hedges.

The castle, which dates from the 16th century, is the most northerly in Britain; to the seaward side the land slopes away to the water of the Pentland Firth with nothing between Mey and the Orkney Islands in the distance. And yet for centuries it was an important home of the Sinclair family, who built it and added the protective walls without which gardening would be impossible in so exposed a position. Evidence of the constant winds is given by the avenue of stunted and bent sycamore trees, which lines the drive to the castle from the passing road.

When the Queen Mother acquired Mey, the castle and garden were derelict, having been unoccupied for many years. The restoration work initially took three years, after which she was able to stay in the castle for the first time. Thereafter, work continued to restore the garden. Despite the inaccessibility she managed to visit the castle fairly regularly in the spring and early summer before spending an annual holiday here of many

weeks beginning on her birthday in August. The garden was always her pride and joy, and, having been brought up in a Scottish garden, at Glamis Castle, she was keenly aware of what was possible in the Scottish climate. At Mey the chief challenge was always the wind and rain, while the proximity of the tail end of the Gulf Stream flowing through the Pentland Firth ensured a relatively mild climate. As a result, if what is planted is carefully chosen to suit the conditions, the results can be surprising, as is exemplified in the walled garden in the height of summer.

Mey is almost a miniature castle, and its romantic appeal is enhanced by the warm pink-hued stone used to build the castle and garden walls. From the seaward side a long stretch of wall extends from the west, where it encloses one side of the walled garden and goes on to join the front of the castle; here, it protects the little area in between, where stone gate piers in the wall frame the unforgettable view out across the sea to the

Orkneys. Further protection on the west, east, and southern sides are given by clumps of sycamores, one of the only trees that tolerate the conditions. The growing season is very short, but an 18th-century description mentioning good crops of apples, strawberries, and cherries confirms what can be grown within the protection of the walled garden, and this is where efforts have always been concentrated.

The fact that the Queen Mother's primary visits were always in late summer and autumn fitted ideally with the growing season, as this was when the garden was at its peak. The walled garden is overlooked by a delightful castellated tower in one corner and retains the ancient hedges that subdivide it into further protected smaller areas. The hedges are an intriguing mixture of hardy fuchsia, elder and hawthorn with privet, dog-roses, and currants. Fuchsias thrive in these conditions and grow into large bushes in many parts of the garden. Neat rows of vegetables are complemented by apple and other fruit trees that are trained against the walls and along the flower borders. Some of the borders were planted with the Queen Mother's favourites, even if success was a challenge for Mey's gardener.

A small formal garden was devoted to the roses she so enjoyed. Other borders are planted with annuals, and rows of sweet peas have long been a feature in late summer. One particular forte is the planting of the display greenhouse against the wall between the rose garden and corner tower; this has always been filled with a dazzling array of begonias, pelargoniums, and other tender annuals.

Between the walled garden and castle is the croquet lawn, where the walls are draped with a mixture of climbing roses. While on the far side of the castle, to the east, is a pair of long mixed borders beneath the wall and one of the garden's best discoveries – masses of brilliant yellow-flowered *Primula florindae* thriving in the damp, shady conditions beneath the sycamores (*see p.183*).

One of the last additions to the garden during the Queen Mother's life was Windy Corner Rosebed, planted to mark her 100th birthday in 2000, two years before her death. But the whole place is imbued with her personality, and, despite the fiercely exposed position, it gives constant reminders of the warm holiday home that it was and now remains for other members of the royal family under the ownership of a trust that the Queen Mother set up. Open on a few days a year, it is a place of pilgrimage for many people who admire the Queen Mother and wish to enjoy the remote privacy of the only royal home that was hers alone.

On a warm day in late summer, when the gardens are traditionally open to the public, it is easy to forget that they are situated on Britain's most northern edge. The garden's healthy survival confirms how well it has been developed and planted both to minimize the damaging effect of bad weather and to take maximum advantage of the relative mildness.

OPPOSITE
The late-summer zenith in the walled garden with rows of annuals fronting quantities of sweet peas, one of the Queen Mother's favourite plants. These are grown each year and thrive in the tough conditions.

BELOW
The enclosing walls protect the vegetables and fruit that grow among the flowers that the relatively mild climate encourages. This produces a late-summer climax, which the Queen Mother enjoyed on her annual holidays.

Laeken

BRUSSELS · BELGIUM

Of all the great glasshouse complexes erected during their heyday in the 19th century, the royal glasshouses at Laeken are among the most impressive to survive. The Crystal Palace and the Great Stove at Chatsworth are gone, as are similar buildings put up for the 1900 Great Exhibition in Paris. The complex at Laeken not only survives, but is in magnificently restored order and continues to provide a source of botanical education through the array of rare and exotic plants that the different buildings contain. And it is not only the size of the buildings, but also the extraordinary variety that makes Laeken so remarkable. The massive complex includes the Palm Tree Pavilion, Azalea House, Mirror Greenhouse, Fern Cross, Rhododendron House, Winter Garden, Congo Greenhouse, Orangery, Maquet Greenhouse, and Dining Room Greenhouse.

The glasshouses were primarily the work of King Leopold II, who in many ways dominates royal Belgian history. Belgium became an independent kingdom in 1830, and Leopold's father was the first king, reigning until 1865. From his accession until his death in 1909 Leopold II enjoyed

OPPOSITE
Looking up into the central dome of the Winter Garden, Laeken's pièce de résistance and one of the most spectacular glasshouses in Europe, for its architecture and plants.

BELOW
An array of tender foliage and flowering introductions beneath a giant agave and palms in one of the long sections that link the main ornamental greenhouses.

LEFT
The foliage of strelitzias and musas in front of massive palm trunks, which confirm the age of these specimens. They were introduced to the greenhouse soon after its construction.

RIGHT
A view through a fern house, where the array of foliage, uninterrupted by flowers from ground to glass ceiling, gives a jungle-like atmosphere.

a reign characterized by projects and activities that belied Belgium's small size and occupied past. As head of an imperial power, especially in Africa, Leopold competed with the great powers of Europe; at home his reign witnessed a series of ambitious civic projects, not all of which got off the drawing-board, but of those that did Laeken was the most exotic.

Ironically Laeken's past was dominated by Belgium's occupiers, and it is interesting that glasshouses were a feature from the start. In 1781 the estate was acquired by the Governor-General of the Austrian Netherlands of which Belgium formed part. He commissioned a castle to be built as his summer residence and created an English park for which the ornamental buildings included an orangery, glasshouses, and a Chinese tower, which survived only into the very early 19th century when it was demolished. The French Revolution ended the Austrian rule and in 1804 Napoleon decided to use the castle as a residence. His wife, Josephine, an enthusiastic

plantswoman, wanted to add to the greenhouses and introduce a number of exotic plants, but sadly her plans came to nought because five years later Napoleon divorced her. After 1815 Belgium was once again amalgamated with the Netherlands, this time under the Dutch king William I, who continued the tradition of his predecessors by building the impressive present Orangery, which replaced the earlier one.

After its occupation by successive rulers of Belgium Laeken was well established as the royal residence by the time of independence in 1830, and Leopold I secured the estate further by adding more land. But his son was determined, as in all his ventures, to have more lasting effect, and the building programme for the glasshouses was planned a few years after his accession, although it did not actually start until the 1870s. By this time Joseph Paxton, who designed the Crystal Palace in 1851, and many others had demonstrated the mastery of techniques of building with a combination of iron and glass,

and they had overcome the practical horticultural challenges faced when having to provide an indoor environment to encourage rare plant species from overseas to thrive. The glasshouses at Laeken not only took advantage of this experience but extended it to new heights.

The most impressive single building was also one of the first to be designed for Leopold by his royal architect, Alphonse Balat, and that was the Winter Garden. This enormous circular structure in the shape of a dome and topped by a royal crown set the tone of monumental architecture that would ensue throughout the complex for over two decades. And yet despite the size, the combination of slender ironwork and glass ensured extraordinary lightness. In the style of the period, as if the plants themselves did not provide sufficient riches, there was further decoration with marble statues, such as the eponymous huntress positioned at

one end of the Diana Greenhouse, urns, and seats, all of which remain in place to this day. Most unusual of all the additions to the glasshouses was the Iron Church built at one end of the extensive complex during the 1890s and clearly a project dear to Leopold's heart. While the church was to be a place of worship it should also fit in with the characteristics of the glasshouse complex and be liberally decorated with plants, including pot-grown exotics and palm trees.

Leopold was as interested in the plants as in the architecture of the glasshouses, and this was confirmed by the fact that he delayed the opening ceremony of the Winter Garden for four years from its completion in 1786 to give the plants a chance to grow to the desired size. Very much in the spirit of the age, he put great energy into sourcing from around the world exotic plants that would only survive in Europe under glass. And one of the great qualities of the glasshouses today is the extent to which they are stocked with plants of venerable age and enormous size, some of them the originals from Leopold's day and earlier.

Among the oldest are the orange trees that decorate the Orangery built in 1817. Many of the trees are over 200 years old and have achieved magnificent size. Other plants from Leopold's time include the various palm trees that add so much to the exotic atmosphere. One of the most significant groups in the plant collection is camellia, many of which have achieved an unusually large size. They date from the 1870s, when most camellias were rarities in European gardens.

As well as the fact that many of the plants are original species, great continuity is retained by the way in which the plants are grown and displayed in the different areas. The long narrow vista of the Great Gallery is still flanked by tiers of brilliant crimson- and pink-flowered climbing pelargoniums, as it was decades ago, and the same goes for the massed Japanese azaleas in the Azalea House, arranged in bold clumps of individual colour.

Over and above any of the individual plants, it is the combination of luxuriance with much originality and many horticultural rarities that create pictures that can be viewed hardly anywhere else. In addition to the pelargoniums in the Great Gallery, the glass roof drips with fuchsias as well as the similar-looking but quite different *Abutilon megapotanicum*. In one area the better-known *Strelitzia regina*, with its brilliant orange and purple colours, mixes with the much rarer *S. alba*, whose flowers are an extraordinary combination of white and black. Some of the most brilliant flowers and a stunning array of orchids grow in this gallery. For many of the large groups of plants, such as ferns, there is an enormous array including some highly exotic ones such as the Staghorn fern from Australia and cibotiums from Mexico.

It is unlikely that such an ambitious complex could survive today if it were not in royal or state ownership, and in recent decades many of the glasshouses have undergone extensive restoration. Leopold II was determined from the outset that the gardens should always be open to the public for a number of weeks a year, and that tradition has been retained ever since. Leopold also insisted on the combination of display, horticultural quality, and botanical interest that makes the glasshouses and their contents so compelling today. After over a century of establishment the manner in which the plants are best arranged for the most dramatic effect has been perfected. But the scientific interest surrounding their appearance and

growing conditions has similarly been maintained and accounts for much of Laeken's importance. Created by an ambitious, well-organized empire-builder with a fascination for both large-scale architecture and plants, the glasshouses have matured into a national institution of great status and considerable significance.

They are also almost unique in Europe, since the enormous majority of the great glasshouses of the 19th century were demolished during the 20th century as uneconomic and too costly to maintain. The fascination with the exotic plants that they housed diminished as the plants themselves became less rare, and the 19th-century enjoyment of great size was replaced by a desire for gardens to be more intimate. So such famous landmarks as the Great Stove at Chatsworth in England were demolished, and only in royal gardens such as Laeken, Kew in England, and Schönbrunn in Austria were such impressive glasshouses not only retained, but kept in the use for which they were originally built. It is indeed fortunate, because in their own way they are as important as period pieces as a great 17th-century formal garden or an 18th-century landscape.

OPPOSITE
The dramatic roofscape of one area of the glasshouses showing the architectural ingenuity of its make-up, with its combination of curved load-bearing ironwork and glass.

RIGHT
Looking along a path in the Diana Greenhouse to the statue of the huntress at one end. The combination of plants and statuary is a distinctive feature at Laeken.

Isola Bisentina

LAKE BOLSENA · ITALY

OPPOSITE

Vignola's superb church illuminates the island and provides the focal point for all aspects of the garden, both the planting nearby and the walks leading away from it and back towards it.

BELOW

An enticing view along one of the garden's wooded paths, with plantings on either side to the focal point of the church dome.

Set on an island in Lake Bolsena, accessible only by ferry, Isola Bisentina is one of the most secretive gardens in all Italy. Although less than 20ha (50 acres) in area the island combines the natural drama of tall cliffs and panoramic views out over the lake with intimate corners of beauty that bear testament to a long history. Following periods of distinction, the land and its buildings gradually drifted into decline; seclusion often meant neglect, until 1912 when the island was acquired by Principessa Beatrice Potenziani del Drago. It was then inherited by her daughter, and since 1986 her nephew, Principe Giovanni del Drago, an architect, painter, and gardener, has carried out an inspired programme of restoration, which has rekindled the garden's beauty without upsetting its Sleeping Beauty atmosphere. The revered Italian writer, Gabrielle d'Annunzio was a friend of Principessa Beatrice's husband, and his quotation over the entrance to the monastery on the island captures this atmosphere perfectly: "It may be that one day I shall carry my spirit to this place, out of the storm."

The island itself was inhabited centuries before the monastery was built. By the 15th century it was under Papal control, and Pope Urban IV used it as a prison for heretics. His successor, Eugene IV, granted the island to the monks of the

Observant Friar Minor order who started the monastery. But real architectural distinction came through the patronage of the Farnese family, who commissioned the main church and a series of six chapels that still stand in different beautiful positions on the island. The high spot was the employment during the 16th century of the great Renaissance architect, Giacomo Barozzi Vignola, who also designed the Palazzo Farnese at Caprarola, to rebuild the original main church that continues to provide the dominant architectural presence on the island.

With great sensitivity Drago has peeled away layers of choking undergrowth and weeds to open up views across the garden areas and to give a wider prospect across the island. His work has also revealed the often ancient trees that provide a natural framework for both the garden and the island's natural topography into which it fits. There is a spellbinding grove of

ancient olive trees and woods of evergreen Holm oaks stretching down to the shore and equally venerable groups of oak, alder, oriental plane, and lime trees.

Into this framework Drago has woven flowering plants such as a luxuriant range of hydrangeas, oleanders, and magnolias, and exotics, including palms, all of which thrive in the islands stimulating microclimate. Neat lawns with paved paths provide the perfect mood between the cloisters of the old monastic buildings and the Vignola church, while on another side of the church is perhaps Drago's most delightful addition, the *Giardino all'Italiana* modelled on the celebrated *lunettes* of early Renaissance gardens by Giusto Utens. These delicate but intricately detailed views of Italian gardens such as Villa Medici di Castello and the Boboli Garden of the Pitti Palace, which were executed during the 16th century, provide graphic detail of the flowers and designs of Florentine gardens at the time when Vignola was working for the Farnese family. A small parterre is enclosed by beds where an array of brightly coloured annuals and perennials are contained by clipped hedges of box and yew. Enormous climbers on the church walls and wisteria over the roof of the monastery building soften the stone architecture.

In the *Giardino all'Italiana* and in other areas of the garden the variety of plants that Drago has introduced is exhilarating. Small pools have been carefully cleared and restored as have some of the smaller temples, and architectural restoration continues on the main church. The result is that the various buildings, the garden, and the island's natural landscape have taken on a harmony that probably never existed to such an idyllic extent in the past. A visit to the gardens takes one from exotic flowers at close hand to the sudden revelation of a view far out across the lake, and in many places the reflections from the water bring a magical dimension to the groves of trees. Indeed the way the garden blends seamlessly with the island's buildings, the surroundings, and the views out across the lake is its most lasting and subtle quality. The contrast with the remote ruggedness of much of the island's scenery enhances the atmosphere of intimacy in the *Giardino all'Italiana* and the garden overlooked by the monastery, and it is this harmonious balance of landscape, gardens, and architecture that visitors take away with them. The sense of discovery on approach is rewarded by the island's secrecy and the surprise beauty that it reveals slowly and only fully for the visitor who takes a journey from one area to another.

OPPOSITE
A study of light and shade beneath the ancient trees in the olive grove, probably planted by monks centuries ago.

BELOW
A colourful mixture of tobacco plants and other bright summer flowers in the beds of the Giardino all'Italiana, *which has been restored since 1986.*

Highgrove

GLOUCESTERSHIRE · ENGLAND

Prince Charles' garden at Highgrove continues a centuries-old tradition in royal gardens in that it is the place where his own gardening ideas and priorities are demonstrated. This is the case with his predecessors and contemporaries all over Europe, and there is definitely a stamp of quality in the advice and designs garnered and in the materials used in the private gardens of royalty. But it is crucially representative of the 21st century for two reasons that underpin the place's whole *raison d'être*; to be a place of privacy and to be developed to the highest standards of environmental husbandry and craftsmanship, both of which are constantly evident. Looking back to when he purchased Highgrove, in the late 1970s, Prince Charles commented: "I suppose I could have gone on searching for the perfect house and garden – a combination of other people's dreams and ideas – but I relished the challenge of starting with a blank canvas and seeing if I could fulfil my own dreams for the garden."

One important aspect of Highgrove for Prince Charles was its status as his own private home in contrast to the official residences where he had spent most of his life. It is a distinction that has had an important influence over other

ABOVE
The Fountain Garden created by Prince Charles at the end of the Thyme Walk, with one of the garden's many specially designed benches to one side.

LEFT
One of the oak temples in the woodland garden designed by Julian and Isobel Bannerman. This one is surrounded by hostas and ferns and shaded by the trees.

royal homes and their gardens. Here was the opportunity for him to develop something in exactly the way he wanted, and to that end, from an early stage, he consulted a number of acknowledged gardening experts.

Originally he was going to be advised by the garden designer and writer, Lanning Roper, but that was prevented by Roper's sad death. Instead he turned to Vernon Russell Smith, a garden designer renowned for his elegant taste and discretion. At the same time his friend Felix Kelly was planning the architectural ornaments of a rooftop balustrade and urns, pediment, and decorative pilasters that would greatly enhance the house's dull exterior. Later Prince Charles would seek the help of two of England's most admired 20th-century gardeners, the Marchioness of Salisbury and Rosemary Verey, who both gave extensive advice on the design but especially on the planting of different areas of the garden. Water-feature and garden-ornament specialists Julian and Isobel Bannerman

have carried out a number of highly individual commissions, from the steel stork that surmounts a column to the pair of classical-style temples made from oak in the woodland garden.

As the garden was, in the words of Prince Charles, a blank canvas, and because he did not have a master-plan, it has evolved in a series of individual areas. These are drawn together by the focus of the house and, more importantly, by the overriding relationship of the garden and the surrounding countryside. For Prince Charles the garden he has created at Highgrove is part of the whole environment. As a result the views to Tetbury church spire and the unbroken transition from lawn to pastures grazed by his cattle and sheep are as vital as the links from one area to another within the garden.

The achievement of privacy was a priority from the beginning, and to this end, to counter the open spaces around the house, the first area to be designed, with the help of Lady Salisbury, was small and filled with ebullient planting and

enclosed by yew hedges. It is known as the Sundial Garden. Today the yew hedges have grown up for the desired effect, and only the planting scheme has changed.

In her book about the gardens of Highgrove, written with the Prince of Wales, with photographs by Andrew Lawson, Candida Lycett Green opens one chapter with a comment that gets straight to the heart of what the prince has sought: "The calm of the garden at Highgrove is a vital antidote to the prince's public life. It is his haven, a loved and familiar place in which he can withdraw from the rest of the world."

Nowhere is this more true than when the prince steps out through the French doors from the hall to the Terrace Garden and the Thyme Walk stretching away beyond. Here, on the west side of the house, is probably the best example of how imaginatively he has transformed the limited and dull garden features that existed when he arrived and how he has also managed to create a balance of formal gardening in the best royal tradition with intimacy. A spreading cedar of Lebanon was retained and now spreads protectively over part of the new terrace and a straight gravel path lined by clipped golden yews, which the prince refers to as "blobs". The transformation here was one of his earliest in the gardens, and again he sought the assistance of Lady Salisbury. As was to become increasingly the case in the development of the gardens, the prince knew what he wanted, and Lady Salisbury provided expert advice.

In front of the house a broad terrace was extended for sitting out. As can be seen throughout the gardens the prince's devotion to the materials for hard landscaping is as keen as his interest in the plants. The terrace was laid with penant stones that focus on a central pool with a low fountain bubbling over an ancient millstone, as a kind of English vernacular version of a Mogul fountain. Facing inwards at angles from the two corners of the terrace are a pair of delightful "pepper-pot" pavilions, which, with garden seats, emphasize that this is an area of peaceful seclusion.

There is no break in the path from terrace to Thyme Walk, which has now become one of the garden's most integral vistas, leading from the house right to the garden's edge with pastoral views out to cattle grazing in parkland. And yet, in a sense true to the Prince's style throughout, the neat formality of the pleached hornbeam avenues and wide expanses of lawn backed by clipped yew hedges is softened by the humps and clumps of numerous different thymes, which have been allowed to grow randomly between the flagstones and setts that have replaced the original gravel; this blurring is heightened by the

LEFT
The view from the house along the Thyme Walk, revealing the imaginative design and sense of progress from the terrace away to the Fountain Garden.

eccentric treatment given to the rows of golden yews. The Prince was advised to remove them but instead he has given his gardeners free artistic rein in their annual clipping, which has produced a vibrant exercise in modern sculpture.

Away from the house, but similarly private is the walled garden, a square enclosed by high old brick walls. Here Prince Charles had been able to develop a hive of productivity and profusion to create an idyllic scene. Traditionally laid out with four large squares divided by paths leading to a central rondel around a pool and with borders beneath the walls, the kitchen garden demonstrates an attention to detail and standard of maintenance that has resulted in an image of burgeoning growth restrained by an integral orderliness. Within neat lines of clipped box hedging are immaculate rows of different vegetables and soft fruit; apples provide blossom then fruit; colour and scent come from the rose and sweet-pea walks; glasshouses bring on plants for the house; and sun-loving perennials spill out from the outer borders over the gravel paths. And all the time, Prince Charles ensures that another of

his passions is maintained, so whether it is the apples, strawberries, or sweet peas, he grows old and rare varieties, or those that have gained a good reputation over the decades as the best tasting or smelling.

Encouraging the survival of threatened species and habitats was the inspiration for one of the garden's most admired areas, the Wild Flower Meadow, which Prince Charles has developed along the curving approach drive. He received advice and wild-flower seed from Dr Miriam Rothschild. Candida Lycett Green has described it vividly: "This is Highgrove's crowning glory. By mid-April there are cowslips, crocuses, daffodils, fritillaries and the first buttercups spreading to east and west beyond the ancient oaks and chestnuts until they merge seamlessly with the fields beyond and the parkland in front of the house…Cutting through the Meadow and linking the Sundial Garden to the Walled Garden is the Tulip Walk. It comes into its own in May. A mown grass path runs between a formal avenue of fastigiated hornbeams (*Carpinus betula* 'Fastigiata'). To either side of it flow purple rivers of tulips…Then the camassias, which seem to thrive on this poor Cotswold brash, begin to creep out into the Meadow in wide drifts of pale blue or the deep bluey-purple spires of *Camassia leichtlinii caerulea*, the Prince's favourite."

As Candida Lycett Green's description confirms, one of Highgrove's great strengths lies in how the different areas of the garden have linked up, no longer appearing like a sum of disparate parts, as the garden has evolved. In whatever route they are taken, there is a sense of progression from the gardens around the house, through the meadow or across the lawns to the woodland garden and arboretum, with discoveries to make in dark, shaded corners, and on to the revelation of the walled garden. It is a garden that achieves the elusive balance of traditional and contemporary, firstly in the way that it is managed and maintained so that as much attention is paid to the salad and fruit crops as to the rare trees and exotic annuals. The balance is equally evident in the variety of buildings and other ornaments as in the plants. But the ornaments never threaten to supercede the richness and quality of the plants and their associations, which emphasizes that this is a garden of horticultural excellence. And, equally relevant, the garden is full of the prince's "favourites", something that stamps it as hugely personal, a place of private experiment and fulfilment.

OPPOSITE
The Wild Flower Meadow at its summer zenith, deservedly one of Highrove's most-admired features and confirmation of the contemporary inspiration behind the garden's making.

BELOW
The Sundial Garden was one of the first areas to be designed, although since then the scheme in the richly planted flowerbeds has changed.

Biographies

Adelaide Princess of Savoy (1636–76)
Italian princess who married the Elector Ferdinand Maria of Bavaria. Her husband gave her the Nymphenburg estate and she was responsible for the central part of the present palace and the original Baroque garden.

Albert, Prince of England (1819–61)
Husband of Queen Victoria of England, born Prince Albert of Saxe-Coburg-Gotha in Germany. He took a keen interest in the architecture and gardens of the various royal homes, especially their private ones at Osborne House, Isle of Wight, and Balmoral Castle in Scotland.

Augusta, Princess of England (1719–72)
German princess from Saxe-Gotha, who married Frederick, the Prince of Wales, and father of George III. Princess Augusta and her husband lived at Kew and after his early death; her interest in botany was the key royal initiative in the establishment of Kew Gardens.

Balat, Alphonse (1818–95)
Belgian architect who was royal architect to Leopold II of Belgium and designed the succession of glasshouses at Laeken.

Banks, Sir Joseph (1743–1820)
English scientist, naturalist, and traveller, who was primarily responsible for the evolution of Kew Gardens in the Royal Botanic Gardens. Banks travelled with Captain Cook round the world aboard *Endeavour* in 1768–71. Later, he was scientific adviser to George III and commissioned the first plant-collecting expeditions for Kew.

Bellotto, Bernardo (1720–80)
Italian-born painter also known as Canaletto who became the 18th century master of grandiose panoramas of continental Europe. He painted a number of views of the great palaces and formal gardens, including Schönbrunn and Nymphenburg.

Borromeo, Count Carlo (1586–1652)
Italian nobleman, whose family owned the island of Isola Bella on Lake Maggiore, where he commissioned the gardens which were restored by his descendant in the 20th century.

Boutelou Esteban (*fl c.*1725) and **Estaban II** (*fl.c.*1750)
Father and son, members of an extensive dynasty of French gardeners working in Spain, who were successively in charge of the gardens at Aranjuez. Boutelou II, in particular, was responsible for some of the designs, and there is a plan of the gardens by him.

Bridgeman, Charles (*d.*1738)
Leading English garden designer who was centrally involved in the early development of the English landscape movement. Most of Bridgeman's garden designs showed an interim style between the French and Dutch inspired formality of 17th-century gardens and the more natural landscapes of the later 18th century. From 1728–38 he was royal gardener to George II and Queen Caroline, for whom he created a new garden at Richmond House, which would become part of Kew Gardens.

Brown, Lancelot ("Capability") (1716–83)
The leading English landscape gardener of the 18th century, responsible for more gardens than anyone before or since. From 1764 until his death in 1783 he was royal gardener at Hampton Court. He made no changes at Hampton Court (he planted the now famous Black Hamburg grape that still survives), but he was commissioned by George III and Queen Charlotte to redesign the old park at Richmond which became part of Kew Gardens.

Burton, Decimus (1800–81)
A leading architect in 19th century England, who designed the two major glasshouses at the Royal Botanic Gardens, Kew – the Palm House and the Temperate House.

Bush (Busch), John (*c.*1730–*c.*1790)
English gardener, born in Germany, who left England to go to Russia and work as a landscape gardener for Catherine the Great. He worked principally at Tsarskoye Selo, and he was succeeded by his son. His daughter married Catherine's architect, Charles Cameron.

Bute, John, Earl of (1713–92)
English statesman, botanist, and garden enthusiast, prime minister of England from 1762–63. A friend of Frederick Prince of Wales, he was tutor to the prince's young son, later George III, and botanical adviser to Princess Augusta, in which capacity he was influential in the establishment of Kew Gardens.

Caroline, Queen of England (1683–1737)
A German princess who became the wife of George II of England, she was brought up at Charlottenburg, and commissioned the gardens around Richmond Lodge which would later become part of Kew Gardens.

Catherine II (the Great) Empress of Russia (1729–96)
German princess who married the future Tsar Peter III. She succeeded her husband as empress after his murder in 1762. She was primarily responsible for introducing the English landscape style to Russia with her commission of the garden at Tsarskoye Selo.

Chambers, Sir William (1726–96)
English architect who was adviser to Frederick Prince of Wales and then his wife, Princess Augusta, for whom he designed the various ornamental buildings in Kew Gardens, including the pagoda. He was influential in introducing the fashion for chinoiserie into England in the 18th century.

Charles III, King of Spain and Naples (1716–88)
Son of Philip V of Spain and Elizabeth Farnese, and grandson of Louis XIV, who during his reign as King of Naples, commissioned the palace and gardens of Palazzo Reale, Caserta.

Charles, Prince of Wales (1948–)
The eldest son and heir of Queen Elizabeth II, who created the gardens around his country home, Highgrove, in Gloucestershire.

Colbert, Jean-Baptiste (1619–83)
Finance minister to Louis XIV with overall responsibility for the management of the king's gardens, especially Versailles during the period of the gardens' creation.

Cubitt, Thomas (1788–1855)
English architect who was commissioned by Queen Victoria and Prince Albert to build Osborne House, Isle of Wight.

De Ligne, Prince Claude-Lamoral (1685–1766)
Belgian prince who created the formal gardens around his family home, Chateau de Beloeil, which had been built by his grandfather.

De Ligne, Prince Charles-Joseph (1735–1814)
Belgian diplomat, soldier and writer who extended the gardens created by his father (*see above*) at the family home, Chateau de Beloeil. He added an area in the landscape style to the original formal garden around the château.

De Ligne, Prince Antoine (1925–)
Belgian prince and present owner of Chateau de Beloeil, where he has carried out extensive restoration to the gardens created during the 18th century.

De Pigage, Nicolas (*fl.* 1750)
German architect who designed the palace of Schwetsingen and many of the buildings in the gardens. He worked for Karl Theodor, Elector of the Palatinate, for whom he also designed the garden and formal park at Benrath in Dusseldorf.

De Vries, Adrian (1545–1626)
Dutch-born sculptor whose work adorns a number of royal European gardens, including Drottningholm, Sweden, where his sculpture group of Hercules forms a centrepiece.

Elizabeth, Queen, The Queen Mother (1900–2002)
Scottish-born wife of George VI of England who had a lifelong love of gardening and was a strong influence on the various British royal gardens, both at the official residences and private homes. Her favourite home, with its garden that she created, was at the Castle of Mey on the north coast of Scotland.

Eyersbeck, Johann August (1762–1801)
German garden designer, son of J.F. Eyersbeck. Responsible for introducing landscape style gardens to both Charlottenburg and Sanssouci.

Eyersbeck, Johann Friedrich (1734–1818)
German court gardener who worked as a designer for Prince Anhalt-Dessau at Wörlitz.

Ferdinand VI, King of Spain (1712/13–59)

Spanish king responsible for important additions to the existing royal gardens at Aranjuaz and La Quinta del Duce de Arco

Fouquet, Nicolas (1615–80)

French finance minister under Louis XIV who created the château and gardens at Vaux-le-Vicomte which provoked Louis into outdoing them at Versailles. Fouquet was imprisoned and died in disgrace

Franz Ferdinand, Archduke of Austria (1863–1914)

Austrian prince, son and heir of Emperor Franz Joseph, who transformed the palace and gardens of his home at Konopiste, Czech Republic (then part of the Austrian empire). His assassination by a Serbian separatist at Sarajevo in 1914 precipitated World War I.

Frederick II (the Great), King of Prussia (1712–86)

King who made Prussia the most powerful country in Germany, but who was also cultivated and created palace and gardens of Sanssouci.

Frederick IV, King of Denmark (1671–1730)

Danish king who originally built the palace of Fredensborg on his hunting estate and commissioned the first formal gardens in the French Baroque style.

Frederick VI, King of Denmark (1768–1839)

Grandson of Frederick IV who completed the development of the gardens at Fredensborg with new areas and ornamental features.

Frederick, Prince of Wales (1707–51)

English prince, eldest son of George II, who died before he could inherit the crown. With his wife, Princess Augusta, he commissioned the original gardens at Kew.

Frederick William IV, King of Prussia (1770–1840)

Great-nephew of Frederick the Great who commissioned important alterations to the gardens of Charlottenburg and added the outstanding garden buildings.

Gameran Tylman van (1632–1706)

Dutch architect who spent most of his life in Poland, where he was the leading exponent of Baroque architecture. He designed the palace at Wilanów for John III, the last Polish king.

George II, King of England (1683–1760)

English king who, when Prince of Wales, decided to live at the house in Richmond Park which had not been used by the royal family since William III. George commissioned William Kent to rebuild Richmond Lodge, and he and his wife, Queen Charlotte, commissioned new gardens.

George III, King of England (1738–1820)

Son of Frederick Prince of Wales and grandson of George II, who established and developed the botanical garden at Kew begun by his mother, Princess Augusta.

Golby, Rupert (1961–)

English garden designer who carried out restoration work and new designs at Osborne House, Isle of Wight, in the 1990s.

Gonzago, Pietro (1751–1831)

Italian painter and landscape designer who worked in Russia from 1792. He combined stage design with painting and landscape work, and was responsible for the area of the Pavlovsk gardens known as White Birches.

Hedvig Eleonora, Queen of Sweden (1636–1715)

Swedish queen, who after the death of her husband, Charles X, commissioned the palace and gardens at Drottningholm, Sweden's outstanding formal garden.

Henry VIII, King of England (1491–1547)

English king who acquired Hampton Court from Cardinal Wolsey and developed the Tudor gardens around the palace, parts of which remain today in restored form.

Hooker, Sir William (1785–1865) and **Sir Joseph** (1817–1911)

Father and son who were successively directors of the Royal Botanic Gardens, Kew, and who played a large part in the gardens' establishment as the pre-eminent botanical institution in the world, which it has remained ever since. They combined expansion of the gardens with regular plant-collecting expeditions, some of which they both went on themselves.

John III (Jan Sobieski), King of Poland (1624–96)

Polish king who commissioned the Baroque palace and garden at Wilanów.

Krieger, Johan Cornelius (1683–1755)

Architect and garden designer who built the palace of Fredensborg and designed the original early 18th-century formal garden.

Le Blond, Jean-Baptiste (1679–1719)

French-born architect and garden designer who studied under Andre le Nôtre. In 1716 he went to St Petersburg, where he worked for Peter the Great; his outstanding work was done at Peterhof before his early death three years later.

Le Brun, Charles (1619–90)

French artist who was principally a painter, but who gained control of the decorative and ornamental schemes in the gardens of Vaux-le-Vicomte and subsequently at Versailles.

Le Nôtre, Andre (1613–1700)

French garden designer who first trained as a painter before succeeding his father in charge of the Tuileries in Paris. He was the most influential garden designer in Europe of the Baroque period and was responsible for the gardens at Versailles. He worked at a number of other royal palaces in France and, prior to Versailles, had created the gardens at Vaux-le-Vicomte.

Le Vau, Louis (1612–70)

French architect who worked closely with Andre le Nôtre to produce the French style that unified a palace and its surrounding gardens – as they achieved at Vaux-le-Vicomte and then at Versailles.

Lennox-Boyd, Arabella (1938–)

Italian-born garden designer based in England who has established an international reputation as a designer of private gardens. She redesigned the garden of Château de Bélvèdere, Belgium.

Leopold II, King of Belgium (1835–1909)

Belgian king responsible for the glasshouses and other gardens at the palace of Laeken.

London, George (*fl.* 1681–1714)

English gardener who established the country's most successful late-17th-century garden business with his partner Henry Wise at the Brompton Nurseries in London. They both worked in different royal gardens, and London was commissioned by William III to create the earliest garden at Richmond Lodge, which became part of Kew Gardens.

Louis XIV, King of France (1638–1715)

French king whose gardens at Versailles were the most influential statement in royal gardening history and were the model for royal gardens throughout Europe for decades afterwards.

Louisa Ulrika, Queen of Sweden (1720–82)

German-born princess, sister of Frederick the Great, whose husband was Adolphus Frederick of Sweden. She made important additions to the gardens of Drottningholm.

Maria Fedorovna, Grand Duchess of Russia (1759–1828)

German-born princess whose husband became Tsar Paul I of Russia, but only reigned for five years before he was murdered and succeeded by their son Alexander I. Maria Fedorovna was chiefly responsible for commissioning the gardens at their home, Pavlovsk.

Maria Theresa, Empress of Austria (1717–80)

Daughter of the Holy Roman Emperor, Charles VI, who ruled the Habsburg empire and made significant additions to the gardens of Schönbrunn.

Marie, Queen of Rumania (1875–1938)

English-born princess, a grand-daughter of Queen Victoria; her husband, the German Prince Ferdinand reigned as King of Rumania 1914–27. She created the small palace and terraced gardens at Balchik (now in Bulgaria) overlooking the Black Sea.

Marot, Daniel (1661–1752)

French Huguenot gardener who fled France in 1685 for the Netherlands, where became garden designer to William III and was the central figure in the development of the Dutch Baroque, exemplified at Het Loo. He also designed the Great Fountain Garden at Hampton Court for William III.

Mary, Queen of England (1662–94)

Wife of William of Orange and daughter of James II of England. Mary shared her husband's interest in gardening and together they created gardens both in the Netherlands and England, notably at Het Loo and Hampton Court.

Masson, Francis (1741–1805)

Scottish-born gardener at Kew who became the first plant collector to be formally sent overseas by Kew Gardens in search of plants. Masson went to South Africa, from where he returned with many new plants.

Mollet, Andre (*d. c.*1665) **and Gabriel** (*d.* 1663)
French brothers from a distinguished gardening dynasty, sons of Claude Mollet. They both travelled to England and were employed as royal gardeners during the reign of Charles II and worked for him at Hampton Court. They designed the *patte d'oie* of lime avenues that remains the dominant feature on the east side of the palace.

Nesfield, William (1793–1881)
English garden designer for whom the re-landscaping of the Royal Botanic Gardens, Kew was the most important commission early in his career. Responsible for the series of vistas which today dominate the gardens' appearance.

Neyelov, Vasily Isanovich (1722–82)
Russian architect who worked for Catherine the Great at Tsarskoye Selo after she had sent him to England for six months to study the gardens. He designed a number of the buildings in the grounds of Tsarskoye Selo, notably the Siberian or Palladian bridge.

Paola, Queen of Belgium (1937–)
Wife of the current King of Belgium, who commissioned the present gardens at the Château de Bélvèdere.

Pedro III, King of Portugal (1717–86)
Portugese king who created at Queluz Portugal's foremost Baroque palace and gardens.

Peter the Great, Tsar of Russia (1672–1725)
Russian tsar who commissioned the gardens at Peterhof to confirm Russia's achievement of sophistication as a European nation and his own power within the country.

Philip II, King of Spain (1527–98)
Spanish king who developed Aranjuez as a summer residence outside Madrid.

Robillon, Jean-Baptiste (*c.*1710–82)
French architect, sculptor and garden designer who moved from France to Portugal *c.*1749 and was responsible for the design of the garden at Queluz.

Roman, Jacob (1640–1716)
Dutch architect and sculptor who was largely responsible for the design of the palace and gardens at Het Loo, where the classical plan was embellished by Daniel Marot's decorations.

Schinkel, Karl Frederick (1781–1841)
Architect and urban planner who was involved in the emergence of the public garden movement in Germany, designed pavilions in landscape areas of Charlottenburg.

Sophie Charlotte (1668–1705)
Wife of Frederick I of Prussia, formerly the Elector of Brandenburg, who was the daughter of Electress Sophie of Hanover, and for whom the garden at Charlottenburg was created.

Tessin, Nicodemus the Younger (1654–1728)
Swedish architect who trained by travelling through Europe and whose work was admired by Sir Christopher Wren at this stage. In his native Sweden his outstanding work was the design of the palace and garden at Drottningholm.

Tijou, Jean (*fl.* 1689–1711)
French-born ironworker, acknowledged as the outstanding craftsman in this field of his generation, who worked in England, and created the great screen of decorative panels at Hampton Court.

Trehet, Johann (*fl.* 1695–1720)
French garden designer, pupil of Andre le Nôtre, who designed the gardens at Schönbrunn, Vienna.

Tuvolkov, Vasily (*fl.* 1710–30)
Russian hydraulic engineer who was responsible for the engineering that produced the waterworks at Peterhof for Peter the Great.

Vanvitelli, Luigi (1700–73)
Italian architect from Naples who designed the palace and original formal gardens at Palazzo Reale, where his work was continued by his son Carlo.

Verey, Rosemary (1919–2001)
English gardener, designer, and writer who advised Prince Charles on areas of his garden at Highgrove, Gloucestershire.

Victoria, Queen of England (1819–1901)
English queen who with her husband, Prince Albert, commissioned the gardens of their country home at Osborne House, Isle of Wight.

Vignola, Giacomo Barozzi da (1507–73)
Italian architect who had profound influence on Italian gardens of the Italian Renaissance through his involvement at Villa Lante and Palazzo Farnese. He also worked for the Farnese family at Isola Bisentina, where he designed the church that stands in the garden.

Von Anhalt-Dessau, Prince Franz (1740–1817)
German prince who greatly admired the English landscape garden and followed this model in the creation of the extensive gardens on his own estates at Wörlitz.

Von Erdmansdorff, Friedrick Wilheim (1736–1800)
German architect and garden designer who worked closely with Prince Franz von Anhalt-Dessau at Wörlitz.

Von Knobelsdorff, Georg Wenzeslaus (1699–1753)
German architect who built the palace of Sanssouci for Frederick the Great, and designed a number of the buildings in the gardens of the palace.

Von Schell, Friedrich Ludwig (1750–1823)
German garden designer who played a central role in promoting the English landscape garden in Germany and who worked at Nymphenburg and Schwetzingen.

Wiedewelt, Johannes (1645–1703)
Danish sculptor responsible for the unique series of sculptures depicting different aspects of Scandinavian life in the gardens at Fredensborg, Denmark.

William of Orange, William III, King of England (1650–1702)
Dutch prince who became King of England. Hcommissioned the palace and garden at Het Loo in the Netherlands and extended the palace and gardens at Hampton Court, England.

Wolsey, Cardinal Thomas (1473–1530)
English statesman who built the Tudor palace at Hampton Court and laid out the first gardens there before it was taken over by Henry VIII.

Wren, Sir Christopher (1632–1723)
English architect who extended the original Tudor palace at Hampton Court for William III and Queen Mary.

Gazetteer of Gardens

AUSTRIA
Schönbrunn, Vienna
Open to visitors
Tel: + 43 1 8775087
e-mail: info@schoenbrunn.at

BELGIUM
Château de Beloeil, Leuze
Open to visitors
Tel: + 32 69/68 95 16
e-mail: tourisme.beloeil@belgacom.net

Château de Bélvèdere, Brussels
Not open to visitors

Laeken Royal Conservatories, Laeken
Open to visitors during April/May only
Tel: + 32 2268 1608

BULGARIA
Balchik, Balchik
Open to visitors
Tel: + 35 9579 72559
e-mail: palace@balchik.net

CZECH REPUBLIC
Konopiste, Nr Prague
Open to visitors
Tel: + 42 0137 721366
e-mail: konopiste@pust.cz

DENMARK
Fredensborg Slotspark, Fredensborg
Open to visitors
Tel: + 45 33 40 31 87
e-mail: nce@ses.dk

ENGLAND
Hampton Court, London
Open to visitors
Tel: + 44 208 7819509
website: www.hrp.org.uk

Highgrove, Gloucestershire
Not open to visitors

Osborne House, Isle of Wight
Open to visitors
Tel: + 44 1983 200022
website: www.englishheritage.org.uk

Royal Botanic Gardens, Kew
Open to visitors
Tel: + 44 208 940 1171
e-mail: info@kew.org

FRANCE
Le Vasterival, Dieppe
Open to visitors by appointment only
Tel: + 33 2 35 85 12 05

Versailles, Paris
Open to visitors
Tel: + 33 1 30 84 74 00
e-mail:
direction.public@chateauversailles.fr

GERMANY
Charlottenburg Schlosspark, Berlin
Open to visitors
Tel: + 49 30 32 09 11

Nymphenburg Schlosspark, Munich
Open to visitors
Tel: + 49 89 17 90 80
e-mail: sgvnymphenburg@bsv.bayern.de

Sanssouci, Potsdam
Open to visitors
Tel: + 49 33 19 69 42 02

Schwetzingen Schlossgarten,
Mannheim
Open to visitors
Tel + 49 62 21 53 84 31
e-mail: info@schloss-schwetzingen.de
Website: www.spsg.de

Wörlitz Park, Dessau
Open to visitors
Tel: + 49 34 90 52 02 16
e-mail: info@worlitz-information.de

ITALY
Isola Bella, Lake Maggiore
Open to visitors
Tel: + 39 0323 305 56
e-mail: isoleborromeo@libero.it

Isola Bisentina, Lake Bolsena
Open to visitors
Tel: + 39 33 88 46 68 69

Palazzo Reale, Caserta
Open to visitors
Tel: + 39 8 23 44 80 84
e-mail: reggiacaserta@tin.it

NETHERLANDS
Het Loo, Apeldoorn
Open to visitors
Tel: +31 (0) 55 577 24 00
e-mail: info@paleishetloo.nl

POLAND
Wilanów, Warsaw
Open to visitors
Tel: + 48 22 842 81 01
e-mail: wilanowm@adm.uw.edu.pl

PORTUGAL
Queluz, Sintra
Open to visitors
Tel: + 351 21 435 00 39

RUSSIA
Pavlovsk, St Petersburg
Open to visitors
Tel: + 7 812 470 2156

Peterhof, St Petersburg
Open to visitors
Tel: + 7 812 420 0073

Tsarskoye Selo, St Petersburg
Open to visitors
Tel: + 7 812 466 6669

SCOTLAND
Castle of Mey, Caithness
Open to visitors for two weeks
in late-summer
Tel: + 01847 851473
Website: www.castleofmey.org.uk

SPAIN
Aranjuez, Madrid
Open to visitors
Tel: + 34 91 891 04 27

La Quinta del Duque de Arco, Madrid
Open to visitors
Tel: + 34 91 891 04 27

SWEDEN
Drottningholm, Stockholm
Open to visitors
Tel: + 468-402 62 80
Website:www.royalcourt.se/theroyalpalaces

Index

Acknowledgments

The publishers would like to acknowledge and thank the following for their permission to use the photographs in this book:

Front cover: Zefa/M Taner
Back cover: Octopus Publishing Group Ltd/David Markson

1–2 Octopus Publishing Group Ltd/David Markson; 4–5 Corbis/© Massimo Listri; 6 left Bridgeman Art Library/City of Westminster Archive Centre, London; 6 right J McDonald, Wick; 7 Corbis/© Nicolas Sapieha; 8–9 Peterhof Museum; 9 Corbis/© Archivo Iconografico, SA; 10 Jean-Pierre Gabriel; 11 Andrew Lawson Photography/Valley Gardens, Windsor Great Park; 12–13 Bildarchiv Monheim/©Florian Monheim; 14 Muzeum Palac w Wilanowie; 15 AKG-Images; 16 Corbis/© Archivo Iconografico SA; 16–17 Bildarchiv Monheim/© Achim Bednorz; 18–19 Bildarchiv Monheim/© Robert Janke; 19 Corbis/© Sandro Vannini; 20 Bildarchiv Monheim/© Robert Janke; 21 top Corbis/© Dave G Houser; 23 Bildarchiv Monheim/© Florian Monheim; 24 bottom-25 Bildarchiv Monheim/© Florian Monheim; 26 Bildarchiv Monheim/© Markus Bassler; 26–27 Corbis/© Hans Georg Roth; 28 Jean-Pierre Gabriel; 29 Bildarchiv Monheim/© Markus Bassler; 30–31 AKG-Images; 31 Peterhof Museum; 32 Jean-Pierre Gabriel; 33 Corbis/© Bob Krist; 34–35 Jean-Pierre Gabriel; 36–7 Hugh Palmer; 38–39 Octopus Publishing Group Ltd/David Markson; 40 Åke E:Son Lindman; 42 Bildarchiv Monheim//© Florian Monheim; 43 Corbis/© Carmen Redondo; 44–45 Bildarchiv Monheim/© Markus Bassler; 46–49 Bildarchiv Monheim/© Markus Bassler; 50 Scope/J Guillard; 51 Bildarchiv Monheim/© Florian Monheim/R von Götz; 52–53 Bildarchiv Monheim/© Florian Monheim; 54 AKG-Images; 54–55 AKG-Images/Reimer Wulf; 56–61 Åke E:Son Lindman; 62 Corbis/© Roger Antrobus; 63 top Bildarchiv Monheim/© Florian Monheim; 64 Bildarchiv Monheim/© Florian Monheim; 64–65 Corbis/© Peter M Wilson; 66–67 Copyright © Patrimonio Nacional; 68–69 Barbara Segall; 70–73 Bildarchiv Monheim/© Florian Monheim; 75 Charles Quest-Ritson; 76–77 Corbis/© Steve Raymer; 78 Marion Nickig; 80 Corbis/© The State Russian Museum; 81 Jean-Pierre Gabriel; 82 Alamy/Robert Harding World Imagery; 83–84 Jean-Pierre Gabriel; 85 Corbis/© Francesco Venturi; 86 Art Archive/Nicolas Sapieha; 87 Alamy/Profimedia CZ s.r.o.; 88 top Zámek Konopiste; 88 bottom Fotobanka/ARTIS – reklamni studio; 89 Zámek Konopiste; 90–91 AA World Travel Library; 92 Corbis/© The State Russian Museum; 93–94 Corbis/© Francesco Venturi; 95 Clive Nichols Garden Pictures/Pavlovsk Park, Russia; 96 Muzeum Palac w Wilanowie; 97 Art Archive/Harper Collins Publishers; 98–99 Muzeum Palac w Wilanowie; 101 Bildarchiv Monheim/© Florian Monheim/R von Götz; 102–105 Bildarchiv Monheim/© Jochen Helle; 105 Charles Quest-Ritson; 106–107 Jean-Pierre Gabriel; 108 Marianne Majerus/Le Vasterival, France; 109 AKG-Images/© Sotheby's; 110–111 Marianne Majerus/Le Vasterival, France; 112 Jean-Pierre Gabriel; 113 Le Scanff-Mayer; 114–115 Royal Botanic Gardens, Kew; 116–119 Royal Botanic Gardens, Kew; 121 Royal Botanic Gardens, Kew; 122 Andrew Lawson Photography; 123 Corbis/© Hulton Deutsch Collection; 124 Andrew Lawson Photography; 125 English Heritage Photographic Library; 126–133 Jean-Pierre Gabriel; 134–135 Bildarchiv Monheim/© Florian Monheim; 136 Andrew Lawson Photography; 137 Octopus Publishing Group Ltd/David Markson; 138–139 Bildarchiv Monheim/© Florian Monheim; 141–147 Bildarchiv Monheim/© Florian Monheim; 147 Andrew Lawson Photography; 148–149 Corbis/© Nathan Benn; 150–151 Bildarchiv Monheim/© Florian Monheim; 152 Paleis Het Loo/Photo Holland; 154–155 Octopus Publishing Group Ltd/David Markson; 157 Octopus Publishing Group Ltd/David Markson; 158 Bildarchiv Monheim/© Florian Monheim/R von Götz; 159 AKG-Images/Dieter E Hoppe; 160–161 Stiftung Preussische Schlösser und Gärten Berlin-Brandenburg/Pfauder/Lindner 2002; 162–164 Jean-Pierre Gabriel; 165–167 Patrick Taylor; 168–169 Andrew Lawson Photography; 170-171 Copyright © Bert Wiklund; 171 Jean-Pierre Gabriel; 172 Corbis/© Yann Arthus-Bertrand; 173 Det Nationalhistoriske Museum på Frederiksborg, Hillerød/Frederiksborgmuseet/ Weiss, Kit; 174 Art Directors/Roy Styles; 175 Copyright © Bert Wiklund; 176 Scanpix Danmark; 177 Copyright © Bert Wiklund; 178 PhotoTresor/Nikolai V Vassilev; 179 PhotoTresor/Yordan Damianov; 180 PhotoTresor/ Yacov Popov; 181 top PhotoTresor/Rosen Dimitrov; 181 bottom PhotoTresor/Yordan Damianov; 182–185 Andrew Lawson Photography/Castle of Mey, Scotland; 186–188 Harpur Garden Library/Jerry Harpur; 189 Jean-Pierre Gabriel; 190–191 Harpur Garden Library/Jerry Harpur; 192–195 Jean-Pierre Gabriel; 196–201 Andrew Lawson Photography.